Harcourt Language

Practice Book

Teacher's Edition

Grade 4

Harcourt

Orlando Boston Dallas Chicago San Diego

Visit *The Learning Site!*
www.harcourtschool.com

Copyright © by Harcourt, Inc.

All rights reserved. No part of this publication may be reproduced or transmitted in any form or by any means, electronic or mechanical, including photocopy, recording, or any information storage and retrieval system, without permission in writing from the publisher.

Permission is hereby granted to individual teachers using the corresponding student's textbook or kit as the major vehicle for regular classroom instruction to photocopy complete student pages from this publication in classroom quantities for instructional use and not for resale.

Duplication of this work other than by individual classroom teachers under the conditions specified above requires a license. To order a license to duplicate this work in greater than classroom quantities, contact Customer Service, Harcourt, Inc., 6277 Sea Harbor Drive, Orlando, Florida 32887-6777. Telephone: 1-800-225-5425. Fax: 1-800-874-6418 or 407-352-3445.

HARCOURT and the Harcourt Logo are trademarks of Harcourt, Inc.

Printed in the United States of America

ISBN 0-15-319102-3   4 5 6 7 8 9 10   082   2003 2002

Contents

Unit 1
- Sentences 1–5
- Subjects/Nouns 6–10
- Predicates/Verbs 11–15
- Simple and Compound Sentences 16–20

Unit 2
- More About Nouns 21–25
- Possessive Nouns 26–30
- Action Verbs and Linking Verbs 31–35
- Main Verbs and Helping Verbs 36–40

Unit 3
- Present-Tense Verbs 41–45
- Past-Tense Verbs 46–50
- Future-Tense Verbs 51–55
- Irregular Verbs 56–60

Unit 4
- Pronouns 61–65
- More About Pronouns 66–70
- Adjectives and Adverbs 71–75
- More About Adjectives and Adverbs 76–80

Unit 5
- Prepositions 81–85
- Phrases and Clauses 86–90
- Complex Sentences 91–95
- Sentence Fragments and Run-on Sentences 96–100

Unit 6
- Commas and Colons 101–105
- Titles and Quotation Marks 106–110
- More About Quotation Marks 111–115
- Negatives and Easily Confused Words ... 116–120

Unit 1 Take-Home Book 121–124
Unit 2 Take-Home Book 125–128
Unit 3 Take-Home Book 129–132
Unit 4 Take-Home Book 133–136
Unit 5 Take-Home Book 137–140
Unit 6 Take-Home Book 141–144
Skills Index 145–146

Name _____

Declarative and Interrogative Sentences

A. Write whether each sentence is declarative or interrogative.

1. Law students and medical students study for hours. _____declarative_____

2. Lawyers and doctors study and learn throughout their careers. _____declarative_____

3. Do you know anyone who has gone to law school? _____interrogative_____

4. The test for new lawyers is long and difficult. _____declarative_____

5. Must every lawyer pass the test before beginning to practice? _____interrogative_____

B. Write each declarative and interrogative sentence. Capitalize the first word of the sentence. End each sentence with the correct end mark.

6. did you know that doctors serve internships
   Did you know that doctors serve internships?

7. an internship is a program of training in a particular field
   An internship is a program of training in a particular field.

8. a medical intern may learn from a well-known surgeon
   A medical intern may learn from a well-known surgeon.

9. can you see the importance of this work
   Can you see the importance of this work?

TRY THIS! Write five interrogative sentences about a career that interests you. Then answer each question with a declarative sentence. Make sure you use correct capitalization and the correct end mark.

Practice • Sentences   Unit 1 • Chapter 1   1

Name _____

Imperative and Exclamatory Sentences

A. Tell whether each sentence is imperative or exclamatory.

1. Talk about your future. _____ imperative
2. Make a list of favorite careers. _____ imperative
3. You could be a famous sky diver! _____ exclamatory
4. Think about being a teacher. _____ imperative
5. Teaching kindergarten would be fun! _____ exclamatory

B. Write each imperative and exclamatory sentence. Capitalize the first word of the sentence. End each sentence with the correct end mark.

6. What a great guitar player my brother is

   What a great guitar player my brother is!

7. how famous he will be someday

   How famous he will be someday!

8. practice hard if you want to become a professional

   Practice hard if you want to become a professional.

9. choose a law career if you like the law

   Choose a law career if you like the law.

10. ask a professional how his or her career began

    Ask a professional how his or her career began.

TRY THIS! Write a paragraph about someone you know who does something you would like to do. Explain what this person had to do to prepare for his or her career. Include five exclamatory sentences. Then write five pieces of advice the person might give. Make sure they are imperative sentences.

Name _____

Punctuating Four Kinds of Sentences

A. Write whether each sentence is declarative, interrogative, imperative, or exclamatory. Then add the end punctuation.

1. Scientists and other scholars publish their work.   _declarative_

2. This work is a long paper on a special topic.   _declarative_

3. What a long paper this one is !   _exclamatory_

4. How can I read these interesting papers ?   _interrogative_

5. Read the published books at the library.   _imperative_

B. Write each sentence. Add capitalization and the correct end punctuation. Then tell which kind of sentence it is.

6. a scientist might write about an unusual rain-forest frog

   A scientist might write about an unusual rain-forest frog. declarative

7. What a long time the scientist's research might take

   What a long time the scientist's research might take! exclamatory

8. would the scientist live in the rain forest

   Would the scientist live in the rain forest? interrogative

9. that would be an exciting place to live

   That would be an exciting place to live! exclamatory

TRY THIS! Suppose that you are a pet-store owner, and one of your animals gets loose. Using the four kinds of sentences, write a newspaper ad explaining what you lost and what people need to do if they see your animal.

Practice • Sentences

Name _____

Extra Practice

A. Write each word group as the kind of sentence indicated in parentheses. Capitalize the correct words, and add appropriate end punctuation.
Possible responses are shown.

1. he will study filmmaking in college   **(declarative)**
   He will study filmmaking in college.

2. he will learn every aspect of making films   **(declarative)**
   He will learn every aspect of making films.

3. practice focusing the camera carefully   **(imperative)**
   Practice focusing the camera carefully.

4. would you want to write, direct, or act in films   **(interrogative)**
   Would you want to write, direct, or act in films?

5. what an amazing actor Alex is   **(exclamatory)**
   What an amazing actor Alex is!

B. Read the following sentences. Add the correct end punctuation to each one. Tell what kind of sentence it is.

6. How many people are on a filmmaking team**?**   _interrogative_

7. Tell everyone to work together**.**   _imperative_

8. What does it cost to make a film**?**   _interrogative_

9. Wow, a short film can cost thousands of dollars**!**   _exclamatory_

TRY THIS! If you could be a filmmaker, what kind of movie would you make? Write a story about one of your films. Include all four kinds of sentences in your writing.

4 Unit 1 • Chapter 1   Practice • Sentences

Name _____

Chapter Review

Some sentences are underlined. An underlined sentence may have one of the following:

- Incorrect punctuation
- Incorrect capitalization

Choose the best way to write each underlined sentence. If the underlined sentence needs no change, choose *No mistake*.

(1) Do you read the music column in the Sunday paper. (2) look at it sometime. It is written by my brother, Sam. (3) He writes concert reviews? Sam loves his job. (4) How exciting it seems. He meets many famous people. Sam works with an editor. (5) the editor suggests topics. Sam likes working on a team. (6) He appreciates his editor's help?

1. ○ do you read the music column in the Sunday paper.
   ⬤ Do you read the music column in the Sunday paper?
   ○ Do you read the music column in the Sunday paper!
   ○ No mistake

2. ⬤ Look at it sometime.
   ○ look at it sometime?
   ○ Look at it sometime
   ○ No mistake

3. ○ he writes concert reviews?
   ○ he writes concert reviews.
   ⬤ He writes concert reviews.
   ○ No mistake

4. ⬤ How exciting it seems!
   ○ how exciting it seems!
   ○ How exciting it seems?
   ○ No mistake

5. ○ The editor suggests topics?
   ○ The editor suggests topics!
   ⬤ The editor suggests topics.
   ○ No mistake

6. ○ he appreciates his editor's help?
   ○ He appreciates his editor's help
   ⬤ He appreciates his editor's help.
   ○ No mistake

Practice • Sentences

Name _____

Complete and Simple Subjects

A. Underline the simple subject in each sentence.

1. Pre<u>schools</u> invite Pablo on Thursdays.
2. <u>He</u> brings his guitar.
3. <u>He</u> plays after school.
4. <u>Pablo</u> plays music free.
5. The <u>children</u> sing along with him.

B. Write each sentence. Underline the complete subject once and underline the simple subject twice.

6. The shakers are made from gourds.
   The <u><u>shakers</u></u> are made from gourds.

7. The gourds' noise sounds like dry leaves in the wind.
   The gourds' <u><u>noise</u></u> sounds like dry leaves in the wind.

8. Many children in the class like to shake the shakers.
   Many <u><u>children</u></u> in the class like to shake the shakers.

9. Three boys play recorders.
   Three <u><u>boys</u></u> play recorders.

10. Martin's friend comes sometimes and plays her recorder.
    Martin's <u><u>friend</u></u> comes sometimes and plays her recorder.

TRY THIS! Think of something you would like to do to help out in your community. Choose one activity, and write a paragraph about it. Then underline the complete subject in each sentence.

6 Unit 1 • Chapter 2   Practice • Subjects/Nouns

Name _____

Nouns in Subjects

A. Write the sentence. Underline each noun in the complete subject.

1. Some people in the group ask questions.
   Some people in the group ask questions.

2. Children from schools and clubs come in, too.
   Children from schools and clubs come in, too.

3. Frank asked about the history of the museum.
   Frank asked about the history of the museum.

4. The house with the workshop was built in 1814.
   The house with the workshop was built in 1814.

5. The garage near the shed was added later.
   The garage near the shed was added later.

B. Read each sentence. Underline the complete subject. Underline the noun that is the simple subject twice.

6. The inside of the museum will be repainted next year.

7. The volunteers on this list will choose colors.

8. The colors for the outside are white and blue.

9. The wall with the mural will be replaced.

10. Leaks from years of rain have damaged it.

> **TRY THIS!** Write a letter to the editor of your local newspaper. Write about a project you think should be done for your community. Underline the simple subjects in your sentences.

Practice • Subjects/Nouns   Unit 1 • Chapter 2   7

Combining Sentences: Compound Subjects

A. Read the sentence. Underline the compound subject.

1. <u>Dogs, cats, and birds</u> need help.

2. <u>Men, women, boys, and girls</u> volunteer at the shelter.

3. <u>Peter, Lauren, and James</u> come to walk the dogs.

4. <u>The director, two children, and one adult</u> spend time with the cats.

5. <u>Steve, Chad, and Brandy</u> still have free time.

B. Combine each pair of sentences to form one sentence with a compound subject. Use *and* or *or* to join the subjects.

6. The raffle will raise money. The auction will raise money.
   The raffle and the auction will raise money.

7. Food and drinks will make the party fun. Games and prizes will make the party fun. *Food, drinks, games, and prizes will make the party fun.*

8. Fran donated books to the auction. Her brother donated books to the auction. *Fran and her brother donated books to the auction.*

9. Steve bid at the auction. Jeanette bid at the auction.
   Steve and Jeanette bid at the auction.

TRY THIS! Are there animal shelters in your community? Write about how stray animals are taken care of in your community. Combine some of your sentences to make compound subjects.

Name _____

Extra Practice

A. Write the sentence. Underline the complete subject once. Underline the simple subject twice.

1. They volunteer for many different jobs.
   They volunteer for many different jobs.

2. Many volunteers from the center coach youth baseball.
   Many volunteers from the center coach youth baseball.

3. Other people help out in hospitals and nursing homes.
   Other people help out in hospitals and nursing homes.

4. Several adults drive buses for senior citizens.
   Several adults drive buses for senior citizens.

5. Any extra time can help.
   Any extra time can help.

B. Read each sentence. Underline the compound subject. Circle the connecting word.

6. Children (or) adults can join the hikes.

7. Sarah, Tim, (and) the group are hiking along the river.

8. Spring, summer, (and) fall are wonderful times to go on a hike.

9. Sparrows, robins, (and) crows fly overhead.

10. Deer, rabbits, (and) squirrels move through the woods.

> **TRY THIS!** Suppose you are a volunteer leading a nature hike. Write a journal entry that describes what a typical day is like. Tell who hiked with you. Underline the complete subject in each sentence.

Practice • Subjects/Nouns   Unit 1 • Chapter 2   9

Name _____

Chapter Review

Read each sentence. Look at the underlined word or words. They may be complete or simple subjects. Some underlined words are compound subjects. Fill in the oval for your answer. If the underlined words are not a complete, compound, or simple subject, mark *none of the above*.

1 <u>Mike and William from our school</u> help children learn math.
- ◯ Complete subject
- ◯ Compound subject
- ◯ Simple subject
- ◯ None of the above

2 <u>Other volunteers</u> spend three afternoons a week helping young students.
- ⬤ Complete subject
- ◯ Compound subject
- ◯ Simple subject
- ◯ None of the above

3 <u>Lisa and Luis</u> from our class come every Thursday.
- ◯ Complete subject
- ⬤ Compound subject
- ◯ Simple subject
- ◯ None of the above

4 The <u>man</u> with the paint roller is Mr. Rodriguez.
- ◯ Complete subject
- ◯ Compound subject
- ⬤ Simple subject
- ◯ None of the above

5 The building is <u>in desperate need of repair</u>.
- ◯ Complete subject
- ◯ Compound subject
- ◯ Simple subject
- ⬤ None of the above

6 <u>Sam, Jesse, and Patty</u> from our block are helping.
- ◯ Complete subject
- ⬤ Compound subject
- ◯ Simple subject
- ◯ None of the above

7 <u>Some wood underneath the paint</u> came off when they scraped.
- ⬤ Complete subject
- ◯ Compound subject
- ◯ Simple subject
- ◯ None of the above

8 The <u>brushes</u> are by the door.
- ◯ Complete subject
- ◯ Compound subject
- ⬤ Simple subject
- ◯ None of the above

Practice • Subjects/Nouns

Complete and Simple Predicates

A. Write the simple predicate of each sentence.

1. Many people work at the dairy. _____work_____
2. Dairy farmers raise cows. _____raise_____
3. Cows produce milk. _____produce_____
4. Butter and cheese come from milk. _____come_____
5. Many markets sell cheddar cheese. _____sell_____

B. Underline the complete predicate once, and underline the simple predicate twice.

6. Cows eat corn and other grains.
7. Farmers buy huge amounts of grain.
8. Trucks carry grain, milk, and cheese.
9. Trucks need gasoline and oil.
10. Resources are important to everyone.
11. Factories turn some grains into cereal.
12. The cereal goes into cardboard boxes.
13. Freight trains travel long distances.
14. Trucks bring fresh food to the markets.

TRY THIS! List some natural resources you use every day. Write a few sentences about how these natural resources help you during your day. Underline the complete predicate in each sentence.

Practice • Predicates/Verbs   Unit 1 • Chapter 4   11

Name _____

Verbs in Predicates

A. Write the verb in the complete predicate.

1. They climb mountains. _____climb_____
2. They sit by waterfalls. _____sit_____
3. Rangers share nature stories. _____share_____
4. Guides explain different areas. _____explain_____
5. Visitors like the area. _____like_____

B. Write the complete predicate in each sentence. Underline the verb in the complete predicate.

6. People share beautiful parks.
   <u>share</u> beautiful parks

7. They make plans for their neighborhood activities together.
   <u>make</u> plans for their neighborhood activities together

8. Voters give their opinions on major issues.
   <u>give</u> their opinions on major issues

9. Businesses advertise products on local billboards.
   <u>advertise</u> products on local billboards

10. The Chamber of Commerce promotes business and tourism.
    <u>promotes</u> business and tourism

TRY THIS! Think about businesses in your neighborhood. Write a few sentences describing what these businesses do to be successful. Circle the verb in each sentence.

12   Unit 1 • Chapter 4   Practice • Predicates/Verbs

Name _____

Combining Sentences: Compound Predicates

A. Underline the complete compound predicate. Circle the verbs.

1. New homes (are) expensive and (use) resources.
2. Timber companies (buy) land and (harvest) trees.
3. Trees (grow) in soil and (need) sunlight.
4. Millworkers (peel) logs or (cut) boards.
5. Truckers (load) the boards and (deliver) them.

B. Write each group of sentences as one sentence. Use *and* or *or* to join the predicates in each compound predicate. Add commas where needed. *Conjunctions may vary.*

6. Architects discuss ideas. Architects draw plans. They work with owners. _Architects discuss ideas, draw plans, and work with owners._

7. Carpenters measure. Carpenters saw boards. Carpenters hammer nails. _Carpenters measure, saw boards, and hammer nails._

8. Plumbers connect pipes. Plumbers fix leaks. Plumbers install sinks. _Plumbers connect pipes, fix leaks, and install sinks._

9. Painters patch holes. Painters paint walls. _Painters patch holes or paint walls._

TRY THIS! Think about one type of worker you would need to hire to build a home. Write a few sentences explaining why this person is important.

Practice • Predicates/Verbs

Unit 1 • Chapter 4   13

Name _____

Extra Practice

A. Underline the complete predicate. Then circle the simple predicate.

1. People (send) messages by e-mail.
2. E-mail (is) quick and easy.
3. Merchants (sell) products on the Internet.
4. Shoppers (order) products from their homes.
5. The Internet (connects) people from around the world.

B. Read each group of sentences. Then write each group as one sentence with a compound predicate. Add commas where needed.
Conjunctions may vary.

6. On-line encyclopedias give information. On-line encyclopedias show pictures. _On-line encyclopedias give information and show pictures._

7. Libraries post book lists. Libraries send messages.
Libraries post book lists and send messages.

8. You can bank on-line. You can listen to music. You can read the news.
You can bank on-line, listen to music, or read the news.

9. Students log on. Students research facts. Students write to pen pals.
Students log on, research facts, and write to pen pals.

10. Computers save time. Computers are fun.
Computers save time and are fun.

TRY THIS! Write a few sentences saying what you think you can learn by using the Internet. Make sure that one sentence contains a compound predicate.

14 Unit 1 • Chapter 4 Practice • Predicates/Verbs

Chapter Review

Choose the best way to write each underlined section, and fill in the oval next to your choice. If the underlined section needs no change, mark the choice *No mistake*.

Nadja is an artist. **(1)** She paints sells paintings and teaches art. Nadja made a website for her art business. **(2)** She hired a website designer asked for her advice. Ellie designed a beautiful website for Nadja. **(3)** People see pictures of Nadja's paintings read about her. **(4)** They about Nadja's career. One page tells about Nadja's ideas on art. **(5)** People from all over the world have seen her paintings. **(6)** Nadja sells more paintings now, makes many new friends.

1
- ⬤ She paints, sells paintings, and teaches art.
- ○ She paints, sells paintings and teaches art.
- ○ She paints, sells paintings and, teaches art.
- ○ No mistake

2
- ○ She hired a website designer asked, for her advice.
- ○ She hired a website designer, and asked for her advice.
- ⬤ She hired a website designer and asked for her advice.
- ○ No mistake

3
- ○ People see pictures of Nadja's paintings and read.
- ⬤ People see pictures of Nadja's paintings and read about her.
- ○ People see pictures or read about her.
- ○ No mistake

4
- ○ They and about Nadja's.
- ○ They about Nadja's career and her family.
- ⬤ They read about Nadja's career.
- ○ No mistake

5
- ○ People from all over the world her paintings.
- ○ People from all over the world, and her paintings.
- ○ People from all over the world, her paintings.
- ⬤ No mistake

6
- ○ Nadja sells more paintings now makes many friends.
- ⬤ Nadja sells more paintings now and makes many new friends.
- ○ Nadja sells more paintings now and, makes many new friends.
- ○ No mistake

Practice • Predicates/Verbs   Unit 1 • Chapter 4

Name _____

Sentences

A. Read each word group. If it is a sentence, write *Sentence*. If it is not a sentence, write *Not a sentence*. Then write if that word group is missing a subject or a predicate.

1. Many Americans love barbecues. _____ Sentence _____

2. The word *barbecue* comes from a Spanish word. _____ Sentence _____

3. Poured sauces for the first time on barbecues. _____ Not a sentence; no subject _____

4. The barbecue grill on a cart with wheels. _____ Not a sentence; no predicate _____

5. Lit the charcoal. _____ Not a sentence; no subject _____

B. Add the subject or predicate that is needed to make a complete sentence. Write the complete sentence. Possible responses are shown.

6. **(Add a subject)** eat barbecued chicken at a picnic table.
   We eat barbecued chicken at a picnic table.

7. Other people **(Add a predicate)**.
   Other people eat salads and hard-boiled eggs.

8. Later, some of us **(Add a predicate)**.
   Later, some of us swim in the lake.

9. **(Add a subject)** fly colorful kites on a windy day.
   My brother and I fly colorful kites on a windy day.

TRY THIS! Write a few sentences about an activity that you and your family or friends enjoy together.

16   Unit 1 • Chapter 5   Practice • Simple and Compound Sentences

Name _____

Simple and Compound Sentences

A. Underline each simple subject once and each simple predicate twice. Then write *Simple* or *Compound* to describe the sentence.

1. People order take-out food at a deli, or they eat there. __compound__

2. Many delis are in cities with people of different cultures. __simple__

3. The Italian deli across the street offers great food, and its prices are low. __compound__

4. This deli delivers food to your home. __simple__

5. I ordered a sandwich for my friend at a deli, but he wanted soup. __compound__

B. Write each sentence. Underline the simple subject once and the simple predicate twice. For compound sentences, circle the conjunction, and add a comma where it is needed.

6. The new German deli sells delicious sausages but I never ordered any.
   The new German deli sells delicious sausages, (but) I never ordered any.

7. Many supermarkets have a deli department.
   Many supermarkets have a deli department.

8. The large markets sell food but they also sell other products.
   The large markets sell food, (but) they also sell other products.

TRY THIS! Write about a special store in your neighborhood. Explain what is for sale at the store and what you like to buy. Use simple and compound sentences.

Practice • Simple and Compound Sentences

Name _____

Combining Sentences

A. Read each compound sentence. Circle the correct conjunction in parentheses.

1. Some restaurants have catchy names, (**but**, or) others carry the name of the original owners.

2. The food in some restaurants is cheap, (and, **but**) some people do not eat in restaurants.

3. Do you eat fried foods, (**or**, and) do you eat well-balanced meals?

4. A diet of fried foods is not healthy, (or, **but**) people like fried foods.

B. Write each pair of sentences as one compound sentence. Add the conjunction that best shows the connection between them. Place a comma in the correct place.

5. Many people feel they are too busy to cook. Restaurants are popular places. _Many people feel they are too busy to cook, and restaurants are popular places._

6. Some restaurant chains are located in Europe. Many Europeans think the food is still American. _Some restaurant chains are located in Europe, but many Europeans think the food is still American._

7. New restaurants open. Some people prefer familiar places. _New restaurants open, but some people prefer familiar places._

TRY THIS! Write about your favorite place to eat and what you eat when you are there. Try to combine sentences to make compound sentences.

18 Unit 1 • Chapter 5   Practice • Simple and Compound Sentences

Name _____

Extra Practice

A. Add the subject or predicate that is needed to make a complete sentence. Write the complete sentence.
Possible responses are shown.

1. New computers **(add a predicate)**.
   New computers are faster and smarter.

2. **(Add a subject)** have computers in their homes.
   Millions of people have computers in their homes.

3. **(Add a subject)** can e-mail family and friends all over the world.
   Computer users can e-mail family and friends all over the world.

4. Computer games and other kinds of software **(add a predicate)**.
   Computer games and other kinds of software are fun and fairly cheap.

B. Underline each simple subject once and each simple predicate twice. Then write whether the sentence is *simple* or *compound*.

5. This area includes a new industry. ___simple___

6. Plenty of silicon is found on Earth, but it remains a valuable material for the computer industry. ___compound___

7. Silicon is an element often found in sand, and people use it in computer chips. ___compound___

8. Many businesses in the computer industry are in an area known as Silicon Valley. ___simple___

> **TRY THIS!** Write three compound sentences explaining what you like about working on a computer.

Practice • Simple and Compound Sentences

Name _____

Chapter Review

Pairs of sentences are combined below. Choose the best way to write each pair, and fill in the oval next to your choice. If the sentence is correct as is, mark *No mistake*.

1 The Statue of Liberty was a gift from France it stands in New York Harbor.
- ○ The Statue of Liberty was a gift from France, or it stands in New York Harbor.
- ○ The Statue of Liberty was a gift from France, it stands in New York Harbor.
- ● The Statue of Liberty was a gift from France, and it stands in New York Harbor.
- ○ No mistake

2 Many immigrants saw the statue from ships, its torch glows for all people.
- ● Many immigrants saw the statue from ships, but its torch glows for all people.
- ○ Many immigrants saw the statue from ships but its torch glows for all people.
- ○ Many immigrants saw the statue from ships its torch glows for all people.
- ○ No mistake

3 Is it only a symbol of friendship is it a greater symbol of freedom for all?
- ○ Is it only a symbol of friendship and is it a greater symbol of freedom for all?
- ○ Is it only a symbol of friendship or is it a greater symbol of freedom for all?
- ● Is it only a symbol of friendship, or is it a greater symbol of freedom for all?
- ○ No mistake

4 The huge statue is a figure of a woman, and she is wearing a crown and robes.
- ○ The huge statue is a figure of a woman, or she is wearing a crown and robes.
- ○ The huge statue is a figure of a woman but she is wearing a crown and robes.
- ○ The huge statue is a figure of a woman and she is wearing a crown and robes.
- ● No mistake

Name _____

Common and Proper Nouns

A. Write whether the underlined words are common nouns or proper nouns.

1. His <u>heart</u> beats fast.   _common_
2. His <u>lungs</u> fill with <u>air</u>.   _common; common_
3. His <u>sister</u> joins <u>James</u>.   _common; proper_
4. <u>Alexis</u> jogs with <u>Sammy</u>.   _proper; proper_
5. <u>Sammy's</u> <u>tail</u> wags in <u>excitement</u>.   _common; common_

B. Write each noun in each sentence. Tell whether each noun is a common noun or a proper noun.

6. He is a lifeguard at the pool.
   lifeguard, common; pool, common

7. He also gives lessons to young children.
   lessons, common; children, common

8. Ryan will learn to swim this summer.
   Ryan, proper; summer, common

9. He kicks his feet in the water.
   feet, common; water, common

10. Some teens are lifeguards at Central Pool.
    teens, common; lifeguards, common; Central Pool, proper

TRY THIS! Write five sentences telling about where lifeguards work and what kind of equipment you think they use on the job. Underline the nouns in your sentences.

Practice • More About Nouns   Unit 2 • Chapter 7   21

Name _____

Singular and Plural Nouns

A. Write the nouns in each sentence. Write whether each noun is singular or plural.

1. We can hear loud beeps and other noises.
   beeps, plural; noises, plural

2. Do you hear a sound by the door?
   sound, singular; door, singular

3. My hearing is so good that I can hear armies of ants marching.
   hearing, singular; armies, plural; ants, plural

4. I can hear squeaks in that direction, too.
   squeaks, plural; direction, singular

5. Do you think they are coming from mice or deer?
   mice, plural; deer, plural

B. Read each sentence. Write the plural form of the noun in parentheses.

6. We can see bright and dull (color). _____colors_____

7. Six (muscle) move the eyeball. _____muscles_____

8. Some people need (eyeglass) for better vision. _____eyeglasses_____

9. (Eyelash) protect the eyes from dust. _____Eyelashes_____

10. You blink your eyes about every six (second). _____seconds_____

TRY THIS! Write about some of the things you could not do without your eyes or ears. Use singular and plural nouns.

22 Unit 2 • Chapter 7   Practice • More About Nouns

Name _____

Abbreviations and Titles

A. Write the abbreviation in each sentence. Write what it means.

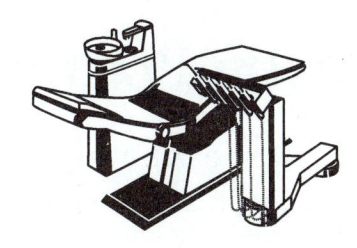

1. His office is on Northern Blvd.   _Blvd.; Boulevard_

2. He has an office on Bell Ave. also.   _Ave.; Avenue_

3. Dr. Cruz filled my two cavities.   _Dr.; Doctor_

4. My next appointment is Aug. 20.   _Aug.; August_

5. Prof. Clark was his favorite teacher at dental school.   _Prof.; Professor_

B. Write each sentence. Correct each abbreviation by adding a capital letter and a period where needed.

6. She works at f. d. Roosevelt High School.
   She works at F. D. Roosevelt High School.

7. The school is on s. Kennedy rd.
   The school is on S. Kennedy Rd.

8. Last mon my older sister went to the school nurse.
   Last Mon. my older sister went to the school nurse.

9. At 10 am the nurse took her temperature.
   At 10 A.M. the nurse took her temperature.

10. By 12 pm her fever was gone.
    By 12 P.M. her fever was gone.

TRY THIS! Write an invitation to a holiday party at your school. Include the time, date, and address. Use abbreviations correctly.

Practice • More About Nouns   Unit 2 • Chapter 7   23

Name _____

Extra Practice

A. Write whether the underlined noun is a common or a proper noun. Then write whether that noun is singular or plural.

1. "Who can do five sit-ups?" he asked our <u>class</u>. _common; singular_

2. We do <u>exercises</u> to keep in shape. _common; plural_

3. <u>Wayne</u> likes the trampoline best. _proper; singular_

4. My <u>girlfriends</u> like to play volleyball. _common; plural_

5. <u>Mr. Ventura</u> checks all the equipment. _proper; singular_

B. Write each sentence. Use the correct plural form of the noun in parentheses.

6. We wear **(shoe)** that fit properly.
   We wear shoes that fit properly.

7. **(Child)** wear sneakers to play volleyball.
   Children wear sneakers to play volleyball.

8. We wear safety **(helmet)** when we ride our bicycles.
   We wear safety helmets when we ride our bicycles.

9. Kneepads help prevent **(injury)**, too.
   Kneepads help prevent injuries, too.

10. Some **(man)** wear wrist guards for handball.
    Some men wear wrist guards for handball.

TRY THIS! Write your ideas for an exercise program for your school. Use nouns correctly.

Name _____

Chapter Review

Choose the correct form of each underlined noun or abbreviation below. If the underlined noun or abbreviation in the passage is correct, choose *No change*. Fill in the oval next to your choice.

Different science **(1)** activitys can show how **(2)** smells travel. The students at Edison Elementary used their **(3)** nosies instead of their **(4)** eyies for this lesson. First, they took four **(5)** balles of cotton. They sprayed perfume on only one of the cotton balls. Then, **(6)** mr Kent, their science teacher, hid all four balls in the classroom. The **(7)** studentes sniffed the air until they found the cotton ball that smelled of **(8)** perfume. Their teacher always does interesting experiments on **(9)** fri at 2:00 **(10)** pm.

1. ○ activities
   ○ activity
   ○ activites
   ○ No change

2. ○ smell
   ○ smelles
   ○ smels
   ○ No change

3. ○ nosses
   ○ nose
   ○ noses
   ○ No change

4. ○ eye
   ○ eyes
   ○ eys
   ○ No change

5. ○ balls
   ○ bals
   ○ ballies
   ○ No change

6. ○ MR.
   ○ M.r.
   ○ Mr.
   ○ No change

7. ○ student
   ○ studenttes
   ○ students
   ○ No change

8. ○ perfums
   ○ Perfumes
   ○ perfumes
   ○ No change

9. ○ friday
   ○ Fri.
   ○ fri.
   ○ No change

10. ○ P.m.
    ○ PM
    ○ P.M.
    ○ No change

Practice • More About Nouns

Name _____

Singular Possessive Nouns

A. Write the possessive noun in each sentence.

1. Miguel loves to visit the forest near Laura's house.   _Laura's_

2. Miguel sees the forest from Laura's yard.   _Laura's_

3. The forest grows near the meadow's edge.   _meadow's_

4. He sees a baby rabbit and then spots the baby's mother.   _baby's_

5. The rabbit's baby lives in a hole with her.   _rabbit's_

B. Write each sentence. Replace the underlined words with the possessive form.

6. The meadow provides the <u>food of the rabbit</u>.
   The meadow provides the rabbit's food.

7. All the <u>animals of the forest</u> depend on it for food.
   All the forest's animals depend on it for food.

8. The forest is the <u>home of the squirrel</u>.
   The forest is the squirrel's home.

9. Deer are the <u>favorite animals of the boy</u>.
   Deer are the boy's favorite animals.

10. The <u>face of the child</u> lights up when he sees a deer.
    The child's face lights up when he sees a deer.

TRY THIS! Write a few sentences describing the wild animals that live near your home. Circle the possessive nouns you use.

Name _____

Plural Possessive Nouns

A. Write the plural possessive nouns.

1. The children's science class studied ponds. _____ children's _____

2. All the teachers' classes were studying the same topic. _____ teachers' _____

3. In the classroom libraries, the books' topics were all about ponds. _____ books' _____

4. Most of the students' reports were about the animals and plants in ponds. _____ students' _____

5. The students needed their parents' permission for the field trip to the pond. _____ parents' _____

B. Write each sentence. Change the underlined words to a plural possessive form.

6. The parents of the girls came on the field trip.

   The girls' parents came on the field trip.

7. The job of the parents was to help the teacher.

   The parents' job was to help the teacher.

8. The wheels of the buses moved up and down over the bumps.

   The buses' wheels moved up and down over the bumps.

9. The students looked for frogs at the edges of the ponds.

   The students looked for frogs at the ponds' edges.

TRY THIS! Write a paragraph about an outdoor place that you would like your class to visit. Circle the possessive nouns you use.

Practice • Possessive Nouns   Unit 2 • Chapter 8   27

Name _____

Possessive Noun or Plural Noun?

A. Write whether the underlined noun in each sentence is singular possessive, plural possessive, or a plural noun that is not possessive.

1. The <u>children's</u> favorite animals in the field are the rabbits. _plural possessive_

2. The <u>girls</u> do not see many rabbits. _plural noun_

3. The <u>rabbits</u> cannot find enough food. _plural noun_

4. All the brush near the <u>family's</u> house has been cut. _singular possessive_

5. Their <u>father's</u> explanation is that the dry plants must be cut to prevent fires. _singular possessive_

B. Choose the correct word in parentheses to complete each sentence. Write the new sentence.

6. Many animals used the **(fields', fields)** plants and grasses for food.
   Many animals used the fields' plants and grasses for food.

7. Cutting the fields removed many **(animal's, animals')** food supply.
   Cutting the fields removed many animals' food supply.

8. Often an **(animal's, animals')** home was in the thick brush.
   Often an animal's home was in the thick brush.

9. Now these **(homes, home's)** are gone.
   Now these homes are gone.

TRY THIS! Choose three animals that live near you. Write two sentences about each animal. Describe what the animals' homes are made of and what their homes are like.

Name _____

Extra Practice

A. Write the possessive noun in each sentence. Then write whether the possessive noun is singular or plural.

1. Jean's cousin Joe loves the forest near the house.   Jean's; singular

2. Jean sometimes calls it Joe's forest.   Joe's; singular

3. The trees' leaves change color in autumn.   trees'; plural

4. Jean looked at her cousins' photographs of the leaves.   cousins'; plural

5. They walked with Joe's family in the forest.   Joe's; singular

B. Write each sentence. Replace the underlined words with the possessive form.

6. The pictures belonging to Nina are mostly of plants and animals.
   Nina's pictures are mostly of plants and animals.

7. There are many pictures of the nests of birds.
   There are many pictures of the birds' nests.

8. Sometimes the shade of the trees blocks her light.
   Sometimes the trees' shade blocks her light.

9. Then she has to use the flash of the camera for light.
   Then she has to use the camera's flash for light.

TRY THIS! Think of five things you would like to photograph. Write a sentence about each one that describes it and explains why it is worth photographing.

Practice • Possessive Nouns   Unit 2 • Chapter 8   29

Name _____

Chapter Review

Read the passage below. Choose the correct form of the noun that belongs in the space in each sentence. Fill in the oval next to your choice.

    __(1)__ class is studying the desert. The __(2)__ librarian is helping him look for books. Some books are about __(3)__ that live in the desert. Others describe the __(4)__ plants. Don wants a book about __(5)__ effects on the desert. He wants to know how people, animals, and plants can all make their __(6)__ in the desert without harming it. He hopes his oral report will hold his __(7)__ interest. He knows that he needs to narrow his __(8)__ topic.

1. ○ Dons
   ● Don's
   ○ Dons'
   ○ Don

2. ○ childrens
   ○ childrens's
   ○ childrens'
   ● children's

3. ● animals
   ○ animals'
   ○ animal's
   ○ animales'

4. ○ deserts
   ● desert's
   ○ deserts'
   ○ deserts's

5. ○ peoples
   ○ people'
   ○ peoples'
   ● people's

6. ○ homes's
   ○ homes'
   ● homes
   ○ home's

7. ● class's
   ○ classes's
   ○ classs's
   ○ class'es

8. ○ report
   ○ reports
   ● report's
   ○ reports'

30   Unit 2 • Chapter 8   Practice • Possessive Nouns

Name _____

Action Verbs

A. Write the action verb in each sentence.

1. Vesuvius towers over the land in Italy. _____towers_____
2. Many people live near the active volcano. _____live_____
3. Geologists watch for signs of an eruption. _____watch_____
4. Scientists research the forces of nature. _____research_____
5. A plume of smoke sits on its peak. _____sits_____

B. Choose an action verb from the words in parentheses to complete each sentence. Write the verb.

6. The volcano ____rises____ about 4,000 feet high. **(rises, is)**
7. Volcanic ash ____makes____ fertile soil. **(for, makes)**
8. Farmers ____grow____ crops on Vesuvius's slopes. **(grow, and)**
9. It last ____erupted____ in 1944. **(was, erupted)**
10. Long ago, Vesuvius ____destroyed____ the city of Pompeii. **(destroyed, or)**
11. Hot gases ____exploded____ from the volcano. **(are, exploded)**
12. The volcano still ____rumbles____ now and then. **(rumbles, every)**

TRY THIS! Draw a picture of an erupting volcano. Then write a three-sentence caption that tells about your picture. Choose exciting action verbs for your sentences.

Practice • Action Verbs and Linking Verbs

Name _____

Linking Verbs

A. Underline the linking verb in each sentence. Write what word is connected to the subject by the linking verb.

1. Mount Saint Helens was an active volcano.
   was connects *Mount Saint Helens* to *volcano*

2. It appeared quiet for a long time.
   appeared connects *It* to *quiet*

3. After the eruption, the volcano became a huge crater.
   became connects *volcano* to *crater*

4. The sky grew dark with ash.
   grew connects *sky* to *dark*

5. The sun looked dim.
   looked connects *sun* to *dim*

B. The simple subject is underlined. Write the linking verb and the word in the predicate that is connected to the subject by the linking verb.

6. Japan's Mount Fuji is magnificent.
   is; magnificent

7. This ancient volcano seems peaceful.
   seems; peaceful

8. Many Japanese citizens feel proud of their mountain.
   feel; proud

TRY THIS! In the library, find a photograph or a painting of a famous volcano. Write three sentences describing the picture. Use linking verbs correctly.

32 Unit 2 • Chapter 10   Practice • Action Verbs and Linking Verbs

Name _____

Using Forms of *Be*

A. Write the form of *be* in parentheses that completes each sentence correctly.

1. I **(am, is)** always interested in volcanoes and earthquakes. _____ am _____

2. The Hawaiian Islands **(are, am)** all volcanoes. _____ are _____

3. The mountainsides **(are, is)** lush and green. _____ are _____

4. These volcanoes **(were, was)** once barren rock. _____ were _____

5. Kilauea **(am, is)** a huge, smoldering crater. _____ is _____

B. Complete each sentence using the correct form of *be*.

6. Even a long time ago, Lassen Volcanic National Park __was__ famous.

7. We __were__ amazed at what we saw last summer.

8. Geysers __are__ jets of boiling hot water.

9. Lassen __is__ a volcanic park in California.

10. __Are__ you curious about Lassen Peak?

11. Lassen Peak __is__ an active volcano.

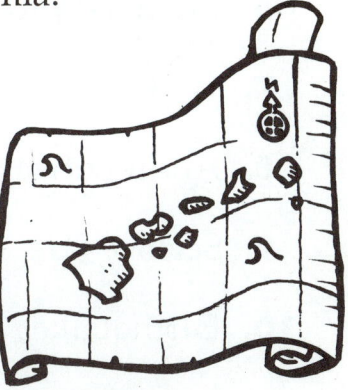

TRY THIS! Suppose you are visiting a volcanic park. What might you say as you look at the sights? Write three statements using forms of the verb *be*.

Practice • Action Verbs and Linking Verbs

Name _____

Extra Practice

A. Write each sentence and underline the verb. Then write *Action* or *Linking* to tell what kind of verb it is.

1. Mount Kilimanjaro rises into the sky.
   Mount Kilimanjaro <u>rises</u> into the sky. Action

2. This mountain is in Tanzania.
   This mountain <u>is</u> in Tanzania. Linking

3. The volcano was active a long time ago.
   The volcano <u>was</u> active a long time ago. Linking

4. Kilimanjaro is an extremely tall mountain.
   Kilimanjaro <u>is</u> an extremely tall mountain. Linking

5. Hikers climb more than 19,000 feet to the peak.
   Hikers <u>climb</u> more than 19,000 feet to the peak. Action

B. Write the form of the verb *be* in parentheses that correctly completes each sentence.

6. I **(am, is)** proud because we climbed Kilimanjaro. am

7. We **(was, were)** on our trip in Africa for three weeks. were

8. Andrew **(was, were)** tired when he returned to school. was

9. Science **(are, is)** easy for Andrew. is

10. Earthquakes and volcanoes **(is, are)** fascinating to him. are

TRY THIS! What are some of the advantages and disadvantages of living near a volcano? Write five sentences to tell what you think. Use at least one linking verb and one action verb in your sentences.

34 Unit 2 • Chapter 10   Practice • Action Verbs and Linking Verbs

Name _____

Chapter Review

Choose the word or words that belong in each space. Fill in the oval next to your choice.

We __(1)__ Hawaii during our vacation. I __(2)__ excited about the trip. We __(3)__ over the Pacific Ocean. Mauna Loa in Hawaii __(4)__ one of the largest volcanoes in the world. Its crater __(5)__ enormous. Visitors __(6)__ the tropical forests. Here, the tropical plants __(7)__ lovely, and the air __(8)__ warm and damp. Orchids __(9)__ in the cinders from the volcanoes. The damp climate __(10)__ perfect for giant ferns.

1. ● will visit
   ○ will follow
   ○ seems
   ○ are

2. ○ is
   ○ are
   ● am
   ○ climb

3. ○ will want
   ● will fly
   ○ is
   ○ am

4. ○ were
   ○ are
   ○ am
   ● is

5. ○ becomes
   ○ eats
   ● seems
   ○ are

6. ● explore
   ○ wear
   ○ doubt
   ○ are

7. ○ skate
   ○ try
   ○ am
   ● smell

8. ● is
   ○ hop
   ○ were
   ○ look

9. ○ is
   ○ lives
   ● grow
   ○ wear

10. ○ are
    ● is
    ○ were
    ○ am

Practice • Action Verbs and Linking Verbs

Name _____

Main Verbs and Helping Verbs

A. Underline the helping verb once and the main verb twice in each sentence.

1. Sponges <u>do</u> <u><u>come</u></u> in different sizes and shapes.
2. They <u>are</u> <u><u>found</u></u> in waters worldwide.
3. A sponge <u>does</u> <u><u>contain</u></u> a skeleton.
4. Water <u>is</u> <u><u>flowing</u></u> into the sponge all the time.
5. A sponge <u>will</u> <u><u>attach</u></u> itself to a rock.

B. Write a helping verb to complete each sentence.
Possible responses are given.

6. This sponge ____is____ feeding on tiny plants and animals.
7. This sponge ____has____ caught food from the sea.
8. Years ago, real sponges ____were____ used for home cleaning.
9. Rubber sponges ____have____ replaced living sponges for this purpose.
10. This package of sponges ____was____ dyed in different colors.
11. People ____can____ use sponges to wash dishes.
12. My father ____will____ wash the car with a sponge on Saturday.
13. Sponges ____can____ become germ carriers.
14. You ____should____ clean them with soap and hot water.
15. Most germs ____are____ killed with soap and water.

TRY THIS! Write a short description of a sponge that is used for cleaning. Make sure to use the correct helping verbs.

Name _____

More About Main Verbs and Helping Verbs

A. Underline the helping verb once and the main verb twice in each sentence. Circle the word that comes between the helping verb and the main verb.

1. A whale's tail is (definitely) used in swimming.
2. The tail will (always) move in an up-and-down direction.
3. The fatty tissue underneath the whale's skin is (commonly) called blubber.
4. Whales have (always) needed air to breathe.
5. Whale watchers have (often) seen whales on the surface of the water.

B. Underline the helping verb once and the main verb twice in each sentence.

6. A blue whale can often weigh 100 tons or more.
7. It is usually looking for food all day long.
8. A blue whale will often feed on codfish.
9. Beluga whales are frequently seen in arctic waters.
10. Some gray whales have typically traveled thousands of miles.
11. They can sometimes leap out of the water.
12. People will often watch for them.
13. Gray whales are normally seen in January.
14. They will usually swim north then.

TRY THIS! Write about what a whale watcher might see from a boat in the ocean. Use helping verbs to describe what he or she might see the whales doing.

Practice • Main Verbs and Helping Verbs

Name _____

Contractions with *Not*

A. Underline the contraction in each sentence. Then write the word or words that form the contraction.

1. Squid don't have hard shells for protection. _____ do not

2. A clam doesn't have a highly developed nervous system. _____ does not

3. Clams can't change their skin colors as squid or octopuses can. _____ cannot

4. Most octopuses and squid aren't thought of as large. _____ are not

5. This crab couldn't escape from the octopus. _____ could not

B. Write a contraction for the underlined words in each sentence.

6. I do not like to eat octopus. _____ don't

7. My cousin has not tasted clams yet. _____ hasn't

8. Dad does not eat squid very often. _____ doesn't

9. We had not tried soft-shell crabs until yesterday. _____ hadn't

10. I would not eat eels or sea turtles. _____ wouldn't

TRY THIS! When you were younger, were there certain seafoods you did not like to eat? What made you not like these seafoods? Using contractions, write five reasons why you would not eat certain seafoods.

38 Unit 2 • Chapter 11   Practice • Main Verbs and Helping Verbs

Name _____

Extra Practice

A. Underline the helping verb once and the main verb twice. Circle the word that comes between these verbs.

1. Sharks <u>have</u> (always) <u><u>used</u></u> their sharp senses for hunting.
2. They <u>can</u> (even) <u><u>hunt</u></u> in shallow waters.
3. You <u>will</u> (typically) <u><u>see</u></u> most sharks on the move.
4. The sharks <u>would</u> (definitely) <u><u>sink</u></u> otherwise.
5. The great white sharks <u>will</u> (usually) <u><u>swim</u></u> alone.

B. Write a contraction for the helping verb and the word *not* in each sentence.

6. Swimmers should not swim near sharks. _____ shouldn't _____
7. The whale shark will not threaten people. _____ won't _____
8. The whale shark does not compare to the great white shark in fierceness. _____ doesn't _____
9. This shark is not easily spotted in the water. _____ isn't _____
10. You cannot see it from above the water. _____ can't _____
11. Nurse sharks do not move quickly. _____ don't _____
12. I have not seen a shark. _____ haven't _____

> **TRY THIS!** Write a list of safety rules for swimmers and divers in waters where sharks can be found. Use main verbs and helping verbs in your rules.

Practice • Main Verbs and Helping Verbs

Name _____

Chapter Review

Some words are underlined. Underlined words may be one of the following:

- **Contraction**
- **Helping verb**
- **Main verb**
- **Word between helping verb and main verb**

Choose the term that describes the underlined word, and fill in the oval next to your choice.

Barracudas **(1)** are found in the Atlantic and Pacific oceans. These silver fish are **(2)** best known for their sharp teeth. Their long jaws are **(3)** filled with rows of sharp teeth. Scientists **(4)** have recognized eighteen different types of barracudas. Divers can **(5)** easily spot these fish. Barracudas can **(6)** swim at great speeds.

1. ○ contraction
   ● helping verb
   ○ main verb
   ○ word between helping verb and main verb

2. ○ contraction
   ○ helping verb
   ○ main verb
   ● word between helping verb and main verb

3. ○ contraction
   ○ helping verb
   ● main verb
   ○ word between helping verb and main verb

4. ○ contraction
   ● helping verb
   ○ main verb
   ○ word between helping verb and main verb

5. ○ contraction
   ○ helping verb
   ○ main verb
   ● word between helping verb and main verb

6. ○ contraction
   ○ helping verb
   ● main verb
   ○ word between helping verb and main verb

Name _____

Verb Tenses

A. Write the tense of the underlined verb.

1. This painter <u>will blend</u> together some red paint and yellow paint. _____ future _____

2. He <u>will get</u> an orange color. _____ future _____

3. He <u>needed</u> this color for a picture of autumn leaves. _____ past _____

4. Then he <u>dabs</u> a paintbrush into the paint. _____ present _____

5. The artist already <u>cleaned</u> the brush. _____ past _____

B. Write the sentence. Use the verb in parentheses that correctly completes the sentence.

6. Early artists **(painted, paint)** on cave walls many centuries ago.
   Early artists painted on cave walls many centuries ago.

7. These cave paintings **(show, will show)** bright colors.
   These cave paintings show bright colors.

8. Today, artists **(use, used)** many new styles and materials.
   Today, artists use many new styles and materials.

9. Tomorrow, we **(visited, will visit)** an art museum.
   Tomorrow, we will visit an art museum.

10. The number of paintings **(increased, increases)** last year.
    The number of paintings increased last year.

TRY THIS! Find a picture or painting that you like. Write four sentences about why you like it. Identify the verb tense in each sentence.

Practice • Present-Tense Verbs   Unit 3 • Chapter 13   41

Name _____

Present-Tense Verbs

A. Read each sentence. Underline the present-tense verb. Write whether the verb is singular or plural.

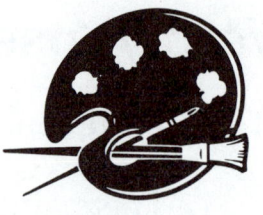

1. Acrylic paints <u>contain</u> special chemicals. ____plural____

2. These paints <u>dry</u> faster than other paints. ____plural____

3. The colors <u>stay</u> fresh over time. ____plural____

4. An artist <u>uses</u> acrylic paints sometimes. ____singular____

5. The paint never <u>changes</u> color. ____singular____

B. Write each sentence. Use the correct present-tense form of the verb in parentheses.

6. The camera **(act)** like a brush.

   The camera acts like a brush.

7. The photographer **(try)** a new camera indoors and outdoors.

   The photographer tries a new camera indoors and outdoors.

8. She **(fix)** a child's hair for a photograph.

   She fixes a child's hair for a photograph.

9. My friend Natalie **(shoot)** action scenes.

   My friend Natalie shoots action scenes.

10. She and other photographers **(plan)** their work.

    She and other photographers plan their work.

TRY THIS! Write about your favorite family photograph. Use present-tense verbs to describe it.

Name _____

Subject-Verb Agreement

A. Read each sentence. Circle the verb in parentheses that correctly completes each sentence.

1. One artist (**sketch**, **sketches**) himself from memory.

2. Other painters (**draw**, **draws**) themselves from photographs.

3. Still other artists simply (**look**, **looks**) in the mirror.

4. This artist's picture (**look**, **looks**) just like him.

5. The other painting (**make**, **makes**) him look younger.

B. Write the sentence. Fill in the blank with the correct present-tense form of the verb in parentheses.

6. The store _____ beads, wool, and other materials for sale. (**offer**)
   The store offers beads, wool, and other materials for sale.

7. I _____ paper crafts best. (**like**)
   I like paper crafts best.

8. Two of my friends _____ the same hobby. (**enjoy**)
   Two of my friends enjoy the same hobby.

9. We _____ scissors, paper, and glue. (**use**)
   We use scissors, paper, and glue.

10. John also _____ jewelry with beads. (**make**)
    John also makes jewelry with beads.

TRY THIS! Suppose that you are a writer. Write about your favorite hobby for a crafts magazine. Make sure that the verb in each sentence agrees with the subject.

Practice • Present-Tense Verbs

Name _____

Extra Practice

A. Write the verb in each sentence. Write whether the action is past, present, or future.

1. A potter adds sand to the clay.   _adds, present_

2. Then he rolls the clay into long, pipe-shaped pieces.   _rolls, present_

3. Another potter will use a potter's wheel.   _will use, future_

4. She shaped two pots yesterday.   _shaped, past_

5. The electric potter's wheel saved her time.   _saved, past_

B. Write the sentence. Underline the present-tense verb. Tell whether it is singular or plural.

6. A craftsperson uses small shells or pieces of larger shells.
   A craftsperson uses small shells or pieces of larger shells. singular

7. Most people glue the shells onto the frame.
   Most people glue the shells onto the frame. plural

8. Then they place it on a flat surface.
   Then they place it on a flat surface. plural

9. The glue dries in about an hour.
   The glue dries in about an hour. singular

TRY THIS! Suppose that you are hosting a television art show for children. Write a few sentences outlining an art project you would guide children to do. Use present-tense verbs.

44 Unit 3 • Chapter 13   Practice • Present-Tense Verbs

Chapter Review

Read the passage, and choose the word that belongs in each space. Fill in the oval beside your answer.

Eleanor __(1)__ stained glass. She __(2)__ pieces of colored glass at a crafts shop. She __(3)__ special tools for her stained-glass work. Eleanor __(4)__ each piece of glass in place with lead strips. A special tool __(5)__ the metal. An iron frame __(6)__ the stained glass pieces together. Eleanor and her brother __(7)__ classes in this art form. They __(8)__ design and stained-glass techniques.

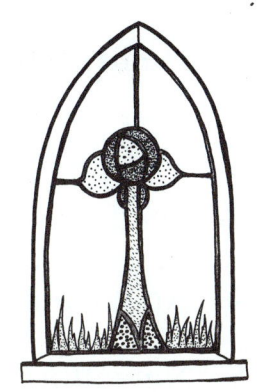

1. ● likes
   ○ like
   ○ likies
   ○ liks

2. ● buys
   ○ buyies
   ○ buy
   ○ buyes

3. ○ needes
   ○ need
   ○ neds
   ● needs

4. ● keeps
   ○ keep
   ○ keepes
   ○ keepss

5. ○ heat
   ● heats
   ○ heates
   ○ heatts

6. ● holds
   ○ holdes
   ○ holdse
   ○ hold

7. ○ takes
   ● take
   ○ taks
   ○ takis

8. ○ studies
   ○ studyes
   ● study
   ○ studie

Practice • Present-Tense Verbs

Unit 3 • Chapter 13

Name _____

Past-Tense Verbs

A. Underline each verb. Write whether the verb is past tense or present tense.

1. He <u>lived</u> in Denmark for his whole life.   _past_
2. Andersen's father <u>introduced</u> him to books.   _past_
3. Readers still <u>enjoy</u> his fairy tales most of all.   _present_
4. Andersen <u>created</u> memorable people and places.   _past_
5. New illustrators <u>offer</u> fresh looks to his stories.   _present_

B. Write each sentence. Change the underlined verb to the past tense.

6. A young woman <u>shows</u> up at the castle.   _A young woman showed up at the castle._

7. The doubting queen <u>places</u> a small pea under twenty mattresses.
   The doubting queen placed a small pea under twenty mattresses.

8. The young woman <u>tosses</u> all night because of the single pea.
   The young woman tossed all night because of the single pea.

9. The young woman truly <u>acts</u> like a sensitive princess.
   The young woman truly acted like a sensitive princess.

10. The prince <u>lives</u> happily ever after with this true princess.
    The prince lived happily ever after with this true princess.

TRY THIS! Write how you would have tested the young woman in the story to see whether she was a real princess. Use past-tense verbs in your description.

Name _____

More About Past-Tense Verbs

A. Choose the past-tense form of each verb in parentheses.

1. The family in *Strawberry Girl* (**live, lived**) on a strawberry farm in Florida.   _lived_

2. They (**tryed, tried**) hard to make ends meet.   _tried_

3. The family never (**begged, beged**) for help.   _begged_

4. The story's events (**unfold, unfolded**).   _unfolded_

5. I (**skimed, skimmed**) through my copy of the book many times.   _skimmed_

B. Write each sentence. Use the past-tense form of each verb in parentheses.

6. Silverstein (**illustrate**) his poems with pen-and-ink drawings.
   Silverstein illustrated his poems with pen-and-ink drawings.

7. My friends and I (**cry**) tears of laughter.
   My friends and I cried tears of laughter.

8. The poems (**tickle**) our funny bones!
   The poems tickled our funny bones!

9. I (**carry**) the book around with me for weeks.
   I carried the book around with me for weeks.

TRY THIS! Write a funny or serious poem on any topic. Write your poem in the past tense. Check the spelling of the past-tense verbs.

Practice • Past-Tense Verbs

Subject-Verb Agreement

A. Circle the correct form of the verb in parentheses so that the subject and verb in each sentence agree.

1. The first book, *McBroom Tells the Truth,* (tell, **tells**) about the adventures of the McBroom family on their new property.
2. Sid Fleischman, the author, (use, **uses**) humor in this tall tale.
3. A tree (**grows**, grow) on their property within a matter of hours.
4. The original owner, Hector Jones, suddenly (**wants**, want) his land back.
5. In this book (is, **are**) many twists and turns.

B. All of the following sentences contain errors in subject-verb agreement. Write each sentence correctly.

6. Amy Wummer, not Sid Fleischman, are the illustrator of this book.
   Amy Wummer, not Sid Fleischman, is the illustrator of this book.

7. In this tall tale, more strange things happens to the McBroom family.
   In this tall tale, more strange things happen to the McBroom family.

8. McBroom's one-acre farm are fantastic.
   McBroom's one-acre farm is fantastic.

9. Why do McBroom need lightning bugs?
   Why does McBroom need lightning bugs?

10. Crops grows instantly on the farm.
    Crops grow instantly on the farm.

TRY THIS! Suppose you are going to write about an adventure that happened to your family. What would the story be about? Write a short description. Make sure the subject and verb in each sentence agree.

48 Unit 3 • Chapter 14   Practice • Past-Tense Verbs

Name _____

Extra Practice

A. Write the past-tense form of each verb in parentheses.

1. The author also **(illustrate)** the book with beautiful pictures. _____ illustrated _____

2. A Native American boy **(follow)** his special dream in this story. _____ followed _____

3. He **(hurry)** up the mountain. _____ hurried _____

4. The boy **(plan)** to paint the great deeds of his people. _____ planned _____

5. He **(use)** the actual colors of the sunset. _____ used _____

B. Write the correct form of each verb in parentheses so that the subject and verb agree.

6. He **(base, bases)** the story on an old Native American legend. _____ bases _____

7. The story **(is, are)** about the first appearance of the bluebonnets. _____ is _____

8. These wild flowers **(look, looks)** like sun hats. _____ look _____

9. People **(call, calls)** these flowers bluebonnets. _____ call _____

10. Texans **(claim, claims)** the bluebonnet as their state flower. _____ claim _____

TRY THIS! Suppose you are retelling a Native American legend. Write a description about how the first sunset might have been created. Check for subject-verb agreement in your sentences.

Practice • Past-Tense Verbs   Unit 3 • Chapter 14   49

Name _____

Chapter Review

Read the passage. Choose the correct word to complete each sentence. Fill in the oval next to your choice.

Once upon a time, an ordinary fly only __(1)__. He often __(2)__ to fly. Finally he just __(3)__ in his tracks. The very sad fly __(4)__ for the first time. He __(5)__ a secret wish. Suddenly a flame from a campfire slowly __(6)__ into the air. As the fly __(7)__ the flame, he changed into a firefly. Different storytellers __(8)__ the story of the firefly. I __(9)__ this one best. The fly in this tale really __(10)__ to help himself.

1. ○ walk
   ● walked
   ○ walks
   ○ walkked

2. ○ tryied
   ○ try
   ○ trys
   ● tried

3. ● stopped
   ○ stoped
   ○ stopps
   ○ stop

4. ● cried
   ○ cryed
   ○ cry
   ○ crys

5. ○ make
   ○ makes
   ● made
   ○ makd

6. ○ climbd
   ● climbed
   ○ climb
   ○ clims

7. ● grabbed
   ○ grabed
   ○ grab
   ○ grabs

8. ○ retells
   ○ retelles
   ○ retels
   ● retell

9. ● like
   ○ likes
   ○ liks
   ○ liekes

10. ○ trys
    ○ try
    ○ tryes
    ● tries

50 Unit 3 • Chapter 14   Practice • Past-Tense Verbs

Name _____

Future-Tense Verbs

A. Underline the future-tense verb.

1. She <u>will replace</u> her record collection next month.

2. The compact discs <u>will last</u> longer than the old phonograph records.

3. She <u>will purchase</u> CDs for her new CD player tomorrow.

4. She <u>will handle</u> her CDs with care.

5. She <u>will store</u> her CDs in special plastic cases.

B. Write each sentence. Use the verb in parentheses to form the correct future-tense verb.

6. This store **(offer)** a choice of recordings on CD next month.
   This store will offer a choice of recordings on CD next month.

7. The owners **(keep)** their cassettes for a few years.
   The owners will keep their cassettes for a few years.

8. This cassette player **(remain)** in stock until next year.
   This cassette player will remain in stock until next year.

9. Soon, many customers **(listen)** to music on headphones.
   Soon, many customers will listen to music on headphones.

10. Customers **(play)** anything they wish before buying.
    Customers will play anything they wish before buying.

TRY THIS! Write why you might prefer a CD player over a cassette tape player. Use future-tense verbs in your explanation.

Practice • Future-Tense Verbs

Name _____

More About Future-Tense Verbs

A. Underline both parts of the future-tense verb.

1. A good recording studio <u>will</u> always <u>have</u> top-quality sound equipment.

2. An audio engineer <u>will</u> probably <u>adjust</u> the sound.

3. The musicians <u>won't</u> <u>record</u> their music with the singer.

4. The editor <u>will</u> quickly <u>correct</u> any mistakes on the tapes.

5. The producer <u>won't</u> <u>forget</u> some copies of the edited tape.

B. Write each sentence, and underline the parts of the future-tense verb. Then circle the word or words that come between the two parts of the verb.

6. The musicians will probably play here tomorrow.
   The musicians <u>will</u> (probably) <u>play</u> here tomorrow.

7. Will the noise bother you?
   <u>Will</u> (the noise) <u>bother</u> you?

8. What lighting displays will the audience like best?
   What lighting displays <u>will</u> (the audience) <u>like</u> best?

9. When will the concert end tonight?
   When <u>will</u> (the concert) <u>end</u> tonight?

10. Will you be here next week?
    <u>Will</u> (you) <u>be</u> here next week?

TRY THIS! If you could be a musician after you finish school, what music would you play? What kind of musical group would you join? Use future-tense verbs to explain your career as a musician.

52 Unit 3 • Chapter 16   Practice • Future-Tense Verbs

Name _____

Choosing the Correct Tense

A. Read each sentence, and underline each verb. Write whether each verb is in the present tense, past tense, or future tense.

1. These awards <u>honor</u> the best singers, musicians, and recordings.   _present tense_

2. We <u>watched</u> the event on television.   _past tense_

3. Some people <u>dress</u> well for the occasion.   _present tense_

4. <u>Will</u> my favorite musician <u>win</u> for top jazz musician of the year?   _future tense_

5. Yo-Yo Ma <u>received</u> an award for his music.   _past tense_

B. Write each sentence. Use the verb and the tense in parentheses to complete the sentence correctly.

6. Leonard Bernstein **(create, past)** different forms of music.

    Leonard Bernstein created different forms of music.

7. My parents **(like, present)** his music in *West Side Story*.

    My parents like his music in West Side Story.

8. I **(listen, future)** to a recording of this musical.

    I will listen to a recording of this musical.

9. You **(remember, future)** the story and music forever.

    You will remember the story and music forever.

TRY THIS! What kind of music does your favorite musical group play today? What have they done in the past, and what might they do in the future? Write three sentences. Use all three verb tenses.

Practice • Future-Tense Verbs   Unit 3 • Chapter 16 53

Name _____

Extra Practice

A. Read each sentence, and underline the future-tense verb.

1. We <u>will look</u> in the newspaper today for the listings.

2. The band <u>won't appear</u> until next week.

3. The concert <u>will</u> definitely <u>be</u> the first show in town.

4. The band members <u>will</u> sometimes <u>wear</u> different costumes.

5. The guitarists <u>will wait</u> backstage with their instruments.

B. Write each sentence and underline each verb. Write whether each verb is in the present tense, past tense, or future tense.

6. I danced last night to the music from a friend's CD.
   I <u>danced</u> last night to the music from a friend's CD.   past tense

7. The music is from a movie and a stage show.
   The music <u>is</u> from a movie and a stage show.   present tense

8. The bands on the CD play the best music.
   The bands on the CD <u>play</u> the best music.   present tense

9. One of the bands first appeared in London in 1981.
   One of the bands first <u>appeared</u> in London in 1981.   past tense

10. My brother will see the movie next week.
    My brother <u>will see</u> the movie next week.   future tense

TRY THIS! Suppose you are a journalist and a very popular band is coming to town. Write a few sentences telling what fans should expect to see and hear. Use present-tense, past-tense, and future-tense verbs.

54   Unit 3 • Chapter 16   Practice • Future-Tense Verbs

Name _____

Chapter Review

Read the passage. Choose the correct verb for each numbered space. Mark the oval beside your answer.

I __(1)__ for dance lessons soon. I __(2)__ only tap dancing lessons. Even when I was a child, I __(3)__ tap dance better than ballet. I already __(4)__ on a pair of great tap shoes yesterday. My best friend __(5)__ tap dance for three years. She __(6)__ in every school musical next year. Next year, she __(7)__ in the show. Maybe I __(8)__ her.

1. ● will register
   ○ registers
   ○ registered
   ○ register

2. ○ wanted
   ● want
   ○ will want
   ○ wants

3. ○ likes
   ○ will like
   ● liked
   ○ like

4. ● tried
   ○ try
   ○ tries
   ○ tryed

5. ○ study
   ○ studies
   ● studied
   ○ will study

6. ○ dance
   ○ dances
   ● will dance
   ○ danced

7. ○ starred
   ○ stars
   ● will star
   ○ star

8. ○ joined
   ○ joins
   ○ join
   ● will join

Practice • Future-Tense Verbs

Unit 3 • Chapter 16   55

Name _____

Irregular Verbs

A. Write the correct past-tense form of the verb in parentheses.

1. Linda and I **(begin)** shopping for folk art this morning. _____ began _____

2. We **(wear)** warm clothes. _____ wore _____

3. We **(bring)** money in case we wanted to buy something. _____ brought _____

4. Someone had **(throw)** out a few paintings. _____ thrown _____

5. They **(throw)** out valuable folk art. _____ threw _____

B. Write the sentence. Use the correct form of the past-tense verb in parentheses.

6. They **(think)** the art was just junk.
   They thought the art was just junk.

7. I **(be)** glad somebody saved the paintings.
   I was glad somebody saved the paintings.

8. Probably someone **(know)** the work of the artist.
   Probably someone knew the work of the artist.

9. The artist **(begin)** his work in a small studio.
   The artist began his work in a small studio.

10. He **(be)** slow to gain the attention of art lovers.
    He was slow to gain the attention of art lovers.

TRY THIS! Write a few sentences that an artist might use to tell friends about his or her day. Be sure to use the correct form of all irregular verbs.

56 Unit 3 • Chapter 17   Practice • Irregular Verbs

Name _____

More Irregular Verbs

A. Write the correct past-tense form of the verb in parentheses.

1. My parents **(take)** us to the Museum of Cartoon Art. _____took_____

2. Some friends had **(give)** them tickets. _____given_____

3. We had **(do)** well in school, and the museum visit was our reward. _____done_____

4. In one cartoon, the wind had **(blow)** a man's hat off his head. _____blown_____

5. In another, two cats have **(take)** some cheese from a mouse. _____taken_____

B. Choose the correct form of the verb in parentheses.

6. Jeff **(rode, ridden)** home from school on his bike. _____rode_____

7. In his hurry, he had **(fell, fallen)** from his bike. _____fallen_____

8. He **(taken, took)** his time after his fall. _____took_____

9. After he had **(did, done)** his chores, he grabbed his cartoons. _____done_____

10. Then he **(gave, given)** them his full attention. _____gave_____

TRY THIS! Write a few sentences about some of your favorite cartoons. Tell what has happened lately to the characters in these cartoons. Be sure to use the correct past-tense form of all irregular verbs.

Practice • Irregular Verbs   Unit 3 • Chapter 17   57

Name _____

Commonly Misused Verbs

A. Choose the correct verb in parentheses.

1. Chris **(sat, set)** down at the table. _____ sat
2. He **(sat, set)** the statues on the table. _____ set
3. First, he had **(lain, laid)** some cloth on the table. _____ laid
4. Then he **(sit, set)** the statues on the cloth. _____ set
5. He **(rose, raised)** from his chair and got ready for the art show. _____ rose

B. If the verb in the sentence is incorrect, circle it and write the correct verb. If the sentence is correct, write *Correct*.

6. Grace ⟨sets⟩ for hours working on her cartoons. _____ sits
7. She ⟨lies⟩ some large sheets of paper on the desk. _____ lays
8. Then she sets her ideas on paper. _____ Correct
9. After a few hours, she rises from her chair. _____ Correct
10. Sometimes she has ⟨laid⟩ down and waited for more ideas. _____ lain

TRY THIS! Write a few sentences describing how a cartoonist draws cartoons. What kinds of materials does a cartoonist need? What does the cartoonist do with these materials?

58 Unit 3 • Chapter 17   Practice • Irregular Verbs

Name _____

Extra Practice

A. Write the correct form of the verb in parentheses.

1. I **(think)** about cartoons yesterday.   _thought_

2. Not all cartoons **(be)** funny.   _are_

3. The cartoonist **(know)** about a news event for this cartoon.   _knew_

4. She **(think)** about the news event.   _thought_

5. Then she **(begin)** a cartoon about it.   _began_

B. Choose the correct verb in parentheses.

6. Roy **(laid, lay)** in bed one morning.   _lay_

7. Suddenly, he **(rose, raised)** and started painting.   _rose_

8. He **(sat, set)** out his paintbrushes.   _set_

9. Then he **(laid, lay)** down his canvas.   _laid_

10. Finally, he **(sat, set)** and painted.   _sat_

11. After an hour, Roy **(lay, laid)** down his brush.   _laid_

TRY THIS! Suppose you are a famous artist. Write a paragraph about a work of art you have created. List words and phrases that describe what you did to create it. Use the correct form of all irregular verbs.

Practice • Irregular Verbs   Unit 3 • Chapter 17   59

Name _____

Chapter Review

Read the passage, and choose the word that belongs in each space. Mark the oval beside your answer.

Rachel has __(1)__ so much in one day. She __(2)__ just this morning. I never __(3)__ about the time. I __(4)__ amazed. She __(5)__ a cloth over the floor. Then she __(6)__ her paints on it. She had __(7)__ her brushes out already. Her fingers __(8)__ as she worked. She hardly __(9)__. By the end of the day, six paintings __(10)__ on the wall.

1. ○ doed
   ○ does
   ○ did
   ● done

2. ○ begin
   ○ begun
   ● began
   ○ beginned

3. ○ think
   ○ thinks
   ○ thunk
   ● thought

4. ○ be
   ● was
   ○ were
   ○ been

5. ○ throw
   ● threw
   ○ thrown
   ○ threwn

6. ○ lie
   ○ lay
   ● laid
   ○ lain

7. ○ take
   ● taken
   ○ took
   ○ taked

8. ○ flying
   ○ flies
   ● flew
   ○ flown

9. ○ speak
   ○ spoken
   ● spoke
   ○ speaked

10. ○ be
    ○ was
    ● were
    ○ been

60 Unit 3 • Chapter 17   Practice • Irregular Verbs

Name _____

Pronouns and Pronoun Antecedents

A. Underline the pronoun and its antecedent. Tell whether the pronoun and its antecedent are singular or plural.

1. Carrie looked at the rain cloud and said, "It is getting closer." _singular_

2. She found Rick and told him to go inside. _singular_

3. Rick said, "I need to put my bike away." _singular_

4. Mother called Carrie and asked her to help. _singular_

5. Then Carrie picked up the chairs and took them inside. _plural_

B. Choose the correct pronoun. Then write each sentence, and underline the pronoun and its antecedent. Tell whether the pronoun and its antecedent are singular or plural.

6. Rick grabbed the bike and put **(it, them)** in the garage.
   Rick grabbed the bike and put it in the garage. singular

7. Rick put both bikes where **(it, they)** would be safe.
   Rick put both bikes where they would be safe. plural

8. Carrie felt the first raindrops and brushed **(them, it)** off her face.
   Carrie felt the first raindrops and brushed them off her face. plural

9. "Rick, **(you, she)** had better come in," said Carrie.
   "Rick, you had better come in," said Carrie. singular

TRY THIS! Explain how you know when it is going to rain. Underline the pronouns and their antecedents in your writing.

Practice • Pronouns   Unit 4 • Chapter 19   61

Name _____

Subject and Object Pronouns

A. Write the pronoun. Write whether it is a subject pronoun or an object pronoun.

1. The rain fell on Rick and soaked him.   _him; object pronoun_

2. Rick watched the drops and saw them form puddles.   _them; object pronoun_

3. He called to Carrie.   _he; subject pronoun_

4. They watched the rain pour down.   _they; subject pronoun_

5. Rick said, "The rain made me cold and wet."   _me; object pronoun_

B. Write each sentence, and choose the correct pronoun. Write whether the pronoun is a subject pronoun or an object pronoun.

6. Carrie brought in some apples and ate **(they, them)** by the window.
   Carrie brought in some apples and ate them by the window.
   object pronoun

7. "Do **(us, you)** like the rain?" Rick asked Carrie.
   "Do you like the rain?" Rick asked Carrie. subject pronoun

8. "**(We, Us)** need to stay inside," said Carrie.
   "We need to stay inside," said Carrie. subject pronoun

9. "This is a good time for **(we, us)** to play our new game," said Rick.
   "This is a good time for us to play our new game," said Rick.
   object pronoun

TRY THIS! Explain what you like to do on rainy days. Write a few sentences about your activities. Use pronouns in some sentences.

62   Unit 4 • Chapter 19   Practice • Pronouns

Name _____

Using *I* and *Me*; *We* and *Us*

A. Write the pronoun in parentheses that correctly completes the sentence. Write whether it is a subject pronoun or an object pronoun.

1. (**Me, I**) was glad when the rain started.   _I; subject pronoun_

2. The news was good for all of (**us, we**).   _us; object pronoun_

3. Ms. Ruiz had told (**I, me**) about the drought.   _me; object pronoun_

4. Mother and (**I, me**) looked for rain every day.   _I; subject pronoun_

5. (**Us, We**) listened to the rain on the roof.   _We; subject pronoun_

B. Write the sentence. Use *I, me, we,* or *us* in place of the blank to complete the sentence. Write whether it is a subject pronoun or an object pronoun.
Possible responses are shown.

6. Dad told Jack and ____ about the rainstorm.

   Dad told Jack and me about the rainstorm. object pronoun

7. Jack and ____ hoped the rain would help farmers.

   Jack and I hoped the rain would help farmers. subject pronoun

8. Dad showed a weather report to ____.

   Dad showed a weather report to me. object pronoun

> **TRY THIS!** What do you and your friends like the most and the least about rainstorms? Write a short paragraph describing your likes and dislikes. Use subject and object pronouns.

Practice • Pronouns

Unit 4 • Chapter 19 63

Name _____

Extra Practice

A. For each sentence, write the pronoun and its antecedent. Write whether the pronoun and its antecedent are singular or plural.

1. Laurie asked, "Dad, do you think the rain will cause a flood?" _____you, Dad; singular_____

2. Dad answered, "I will not know until later." _____I, Dad; singular_____

3. Dad and Laurie agreed that they hoped the storm would be over soon. _____they, Dad and Laurie; plural_____

4. Our neighbors remembered they had problems during the last flood. _____they, neighbors; plural_____

5. Laurie said she was going to turn on the news again. _____she, Laurie; singular_____

B. Write the pronoun in parentheses that correctly completes the sentence. Write whether it is a subject pronoun or an object pronoun.

6. Dad told **(I, me)** to watch the news. _____me; object pronoun_____

7. Then Mom told **(us, we)** about the flood warning. _____us; object pronoun_____

8. **(I, me)** talked to the neighbors on the porch. _____I; subject pronoun_____

TRY THIS! Suppose you are a weather forecaster. Write a short weather report for a television news show. You can report good weather or a storm. Use the pronouns *us* and *we*.

Name _____

Chapter Review

Read the passage, and choose the correct pronoun for each blank.

When Gino and I came home, __(1)__ were dripping wet. A car driving through a puddle had splashed __(2)__. The weather report on television worried __(3)__. __(4)__ needed the rain, but too much had fallen too fast. Already water covered some streets, but __(5)__ was not very deep yet. People could drive cars, but __(6)__ had to be careful. The weather forecaster said __(7)__ did not know yet whether the rain would cause a flood. A reporter was sending __(8)__ some information.

1. ● we
   ○ us
   ○ I
   ○ he

2. ○ we
   ● us
   ○ I
   ○ he

3. ○ we
   ● us
   ○ I
   ○ he

4. ○ Me
   ○ Him
   ● We
   ○ Them

5. ○ I
   ○ they
   ○ them
   ● it

6. ○ he
   ○ it
   ○ them
   ● they

7. ○ her
   ○ him
   ● she
   ○ it

8. ● her
   ○ she
   ○ they
   ○ he

Practice • Pronouns

Unit 4 • Chapter 19   65

Name _____

Possessive Pronouns

A. Write the possessive pronoun in each sentence.

1. Our projects are all lined up on one wall in the classroom. _____ Our

2. "Where is yours?" I asked Jenna. _____ yours

3. "Mine is the one with the sixteen moons of Jupiter," she said. _____ Mine

4. Jenna picked up her model and showed me the different moons. _____ her

5. Some of its moons are huge! _____ its

B. Write the sentence, and underline each possessive pronoun. Draw an arrow from each pronoun to the noun that follows it. If the possessive pronoun stands alone, write *Stands alone*.

6. Jake entered the room with his project.
   Jake entered the room with his project.

7. Jenna picked up hers and moved it for him.
   Jenna picked up hers and moved it for him. Stands alone

8. He placed his next to hers.
   He placed his next to hers. Both stand alone.

9. Both of their projects were on Jupiter.
   Both of their projects were on Jupiter.

10. Jake illustrated its atmosphere.
    Jake illustrated its atmosphere.

TRY THIS! Write a few sentences about another planet you would like to visit and why. Make sure to use at least two possessive pronouns.

Practice • More About Pronouns

Name _____

Contractions with Pronouns

A. Write each sentence, and replace the words in parentheses with a contraction.

1. Ella said (she would) make a model of Mars's moons.
   Ella said she'd make a model of Mars's moons.

2. (She will) suspend them by wire when she gets to class.
   She'll suspend them by wire when she gets to class.

3. (I will) help her set up the display.
   I'll help her set up the display.

4. (It will) show that the bigger moon is called Phobos.
   It'll show that the bigger moon is called Phobos.

5. (It is) clear that Deimos is the smaller moon.
   It's clear that Deimos is the smaller moon.

B. Underline the contraction in each sentence. Write the two words that make up each contraction.

6. I've finished my models at last. — I have
7. They've taken me a long time to make. — They have
8. They're models of Saturn and its moons. — They are
9. They'll show that Saturn has rings. — They will
10. I'm going to explain that Saturn is the second largest planet. — I am

TRY THIS! Write five sentences about what you and your friends would do on a spaceship to keep yourselves busy. Circle all contractions.

Practice • More About Pronouns

Name _____

Homophones

A. For each sentence, decide which word in parentheses is correct. Write each sentence with the correct word.

1. Is (**your, you're**) father going to use his telescope tonight?
   Is your father going to use his telescope tonight?

2. Mars is over (**their, there**). *Mars is over there.*

3. We cannot see (**its, it's**) moons through our telescope.
   We cannot see its moons through our telescope.

4. (**Your, You're**) sure we cannot see Pluto and Neptune without a telescope? *You're sure we cannot see Pluto and Neptune without a telescope?*

5. (**There, They're**) too far away. *They're too far away.*

B. Read each sentence. Fill in the blank by choosing the word from the box that makes the most sense.

| its | it's | your | you're | their | they're | there |

6. According to the model, __*it's*__ the largest planet in our solar system.

7. Ellen and Ray brought __*their*__ projects in early.

8. __*They're*__ both very proud of their work.

9. Ray's model has __*its*__ own power pack.

10. __*You're*__ going to see his model of Earth turn.

TRY THIS! Write a few sentences explaining what you think the stars would look like through a telescope. Use at least three of the following: *it's, its, you're, your, there, their,* and *they're*.

68 Unit 4 • Chapter 20   Practice • More About Pronouns

Name _____

Extra Practice

A. Write each sentence, and underline each possessive pronoun. Draw an arrow from each pronoun to the noun that follows it. If the possessive pronoun stands alone, write *Stands alone*.

1. They especially liked the way I made its rings.
   They especially liked the way I made its rings.

2. Jupiter and Uranus have rings, but theirs are fainter.
   Jupiter and Uranus have rings, but theirs are fainter. Stands alone

3. Jake painted faint rings around his model of Jupiter.
   Jake painted faint rings around his model of Jupiter.

4. His did not give as much information as mine.
   His did not give as much information as mine. Both stand alone

5. Ours stood out as the most colorful displays.
   Ours stood out as the most colorful displays. Stands alone

B. Read each sentence. Circle the correct word in parentheses to complete the sentence.

6. (Its, **It's**) the closest to Earth of all the planets.

7. (Your, **You're**) curious about Venus?

8. (**My**, Mine) teacher tells us (**it's**, its) called Earth's twin.

9. (Their, **They're**) similar in size.

10. Venus is so hot that you would not want to visit (their, **there**)!

TRY THIS! Suppose you are moving to another planet. Write a few sentences saying what you would bring with you and why these things would be useful. Use pronouns in your description.

Practice • More About Pronouns   Unit 4 • Chapter 20   69

Name _____

Chapter Review

Choose the correct way to write each underlined sentence, and fill in the oval next to your choice. If the underlined sentence needs no change, mark the choice *No mistake*.

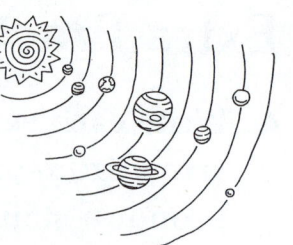

(1) I asked mine neighbors about the planet Pluto. (2) They told me its about 3,666,200,000 miles from the sun! (3) It's far out their in space! (4) The Greens brought out they're solar system map. Ms. Green said, "Pluto is usually the planet that is the farthest away. (5) Every 248 years it's closer to the sun than Neptune. (6) His orbit stays like that for 20 years. It was this way from 1979 until 1999."

1. ○ I asked theirs neighbors about the planet Pluto.
   ● I asked my neighbors about the planet Pluto.
   ○ I asked my about the planet Pluto.
   ○ No mistake

2. ● They told me it's about 3,666,200,000 miles from the sun!
   ○ They told me it about 3,666,200,000 miles from the sun!
   ○ They told me there about 3,666,200,000 miles from the sun!
   ○ No mistake

3. ● It's far out there in space!
   ○ Its far out their in space!
   ○ It's far out they're in space!
   ○ No mistake

4. ● The Greens brought out their solar system map.
   ○ The Greens brought out there solar system map.
   ○ The Greens brought out theirs.
   ○ No mistake

5. ○ Every 248 years its closer to the sun than Neptune.
   ○ Every 248 years their closer to the sun than Neptune.
   ○ Every 248 years it closer to the sun than Neptune.
   ● No mistake

6. ○ It orbit stays like that for 20 years.
   ○ It's orbit stays like that for 20 years.
   ● Its orbit stays like that for 20 years.
   ○ No mistake

70   Unit 4 • Chapter 20   Practice • More About Pronouns

Name _____

Adjectives

A. Underline each adjective, including articles. Draw an arrow from each adjective to the word the adjective describes.

1. It was <u>an</u> <u>empty</u> lot.

2. People in the community pulled <u>the</u> <u>overgrown</u> weeds.

3. <u>Some</u> people planted <u>pretty</u> flowers.

4. <u>The</u> <u>French</u> lilacs will grow to <u>twenty</u> feet.

5. <u>Other</u> people planted <u>different</u> seeds.

B. Write each sentence. Underline the adjective. Then write whether the adjective tells *what kind, how many,* or *which one.*

6. Orchids grow in warm climates.
   Orchids grow in <u>warm</u> climates. what kind

7. Growers produce new forms of flowers.
   Growers produce <u>new</u> forms of flowers. what kind

8. Three petals are on your flower.
   <u>Three</u> petals are on your flower. how many

9. Look at these flowers.
   Look at <u>these</u> flowers. which one

10. I like white orchids.
    I like <u>white</u> orchids. what kind

TRY THIS! Write a description of the flowers you would grow in a garden. Use adjectives to describe the flowers.

Practice • Adjectives and Adverbs   Unit 4 • Chapter 22   71

Name _____

Adverbs

A. Write the adverb and the verb it describes. Underline the verb the adverb describes.

1. The seeds are packed loosely in an envelope.   loosely; packed

2. Gardeners plant the seeds early in the growing season.   early; plant

3. They water the ground often.   often; water

4. They always pull any weeds.   always; pull

5. The plants grow quickly in the warm sun.   quickly; grow

B. Write each sentence. Underline the adverb. Then write whether the adverb tells *where, when,* or *how*.

6. I picked some flowers yesterday.
   I picked some flowers yesterday. when

7. I arranged the roses carefully in a basket.
   I arranged the roses carefully in a basket. how

8. The basket suddenly fell.
   The basket suddenly fell. how

9. The flowers tumbled out.
   The flowers tumbled out. where

TRY THIS! Write what might happen to flowers in a window box during a heavy rainfall. Use adverbs.

72 Unit 4 • Chapter 22   Practice • Adjectives and Adverbs

Name _____

Adjective or Adverb?

A. Write each sentence. Add the adjective and adverb in parentheses to each sentence.
Possible responses are shown.

1. The glass allows the sunlight in.   (clear, naturally)

   The clear glass allows the sunlight in naturally.

2. In winter, a greenhouse uses lights.   (artificial, also)

   In winter, a greenhouse uses artificial lights also.

3. In summer, fans blow air.   (cool, around)

   In summer, fans blow cool air around.

4. Plants such as orchids can grow.   (delicate, inside)

   Plants such as delicate orchids can grow inside.

5. Besides light, plants need warmth and moisture.   (these, usually)

   Besides light, these plants usually need warmth and moisture.

B. Underline each adjective and circle each adverb in the sentence.

6. This plant has one blossom, and it stands (alone).

7. The taller sunflowers (easily) reach a height of twelve feet.

8. The long stem (usually) bends in the direction of the sun.

9. Many people (often) eat the raw seeds.

10. (Today,) cooks use the healthful oil of the tiny seed.

TRY THIS! Write about an imaginary visit to a greenhouse. What might you see, smell, hear, and feel there? Use adjectives and adverbs correctly.

Practice • Adjectives and Adverbs   Unit 4 • Chapter 22   73

Name _____

Extra Practice

A. Write the adjectives in each sentence. Include articles and proper adjectives.

1. Spices are from flavorful fruits and seeds of certain plants. _____ flavorful, certain _____

2. The different spices have wonderful odors. _____ The, different, wonderful _____

3. The yellow seed has a sharp flavor. _____ The, yellow, a, sharp _____

4. Some cooks sprinkle tasty garlic on food. _____ Some, tasty _____

5. Black pepper is an Indian spice. _____ Black, an, Indian _____

B. Write the adverb and the word or words each adverb modifies. Underline the word or words the adverb describes.

6. Some people grow basil outdoors. _____ outdoors; grow _____

7. They will also plant this herb in indoor pots. _____ also; will plant _____

8. Basil grows well in both areas. _____ well; grows _____

9. Yesterday I crushed the basil leaves. _____ Yesterday; crushed _____

10. I season the fish with this herb now. _____ now; season _____

TRY THIS! Describe the sights, sounds, and smells of a kitchen where someone is busy cooking. Use adjectives and adverbs correctly.

Name _____

Chapter Review

Each of the following numbered items is a complete sentence broken into three lines. If you see a mistake in a sentence, fill in the oval of the line with the mistake. If the whole sentence is correct, mark *No mistake*.

1. ○ Vanilla is a deliciously
   ○ flavoring for many
   ○ types of foods.
   ○ No mistake

2. ○ I always liked
   ○ vanilla ice cream
   ○ the best.
   ○ No mistake

3. ○ No pudding is
   ○ more tastefully than
   ○ vanilla pudding.
   ○ No mistake

4. ○ An vanilla flavoring
   ○ in cake frosting
   ○ is delicious.
   ○ No mistake

5. ○ Vanilla flavoring is
   ○ usual used in
   ○ some soft drinks.
   ○ No mistake

6. ○ A vanilla flavoring
   ○ goes good with
   ○ many baked goods.
   ○ No mistake

7. ○ Farmers grow
   ○ a Tahitian vanilla beans
   ○ in South America.
   ○ No mistake

8. ○ The cherry flavor
   ○ is used in some
   ○ soups and perfumes.
   ○ No mistake

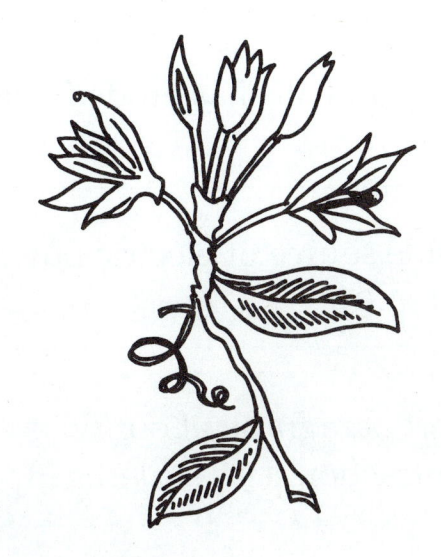

Practice • Adjectives and Adverbs   Unit 4 • Chapter 22   75

Name _____

Other Kinds of Adverbs

A. Write the word that each underlined adverb modifies. Then write whether that word is an adjective or another adverb.

1. Niagara Falls is one of the <u>most</u> spectacular natural wonders in North America. _____ spectacular, adjective _____

2. I would like to visit these waterfalls <u>more</u> often.
   _____ often, adverb _____

3. Niagara Falls is divided into two <u>completely</u> separate falls.
   _____ separate, adjective _____

4. The Horseshoe Falls in Canada flows <u>more</u> forcefully than the American Falls. _____ forcefully, adverb _____

5. The American Falls features the <u>equally</u> breathtaking Bridal Veil Falls and Cave of the Winds. _____ breathtaking, adjective _____

B. Write the sentence. Underline the adverb that modifies an adjective or another adverb in each sentence.

6. The constantly flowing water tumbles to the rocks below.
   The <u>constantly</u> flowing water tumbles to the rocks below.

7. The rocky edge under Niagara Falls has eroded very slowly.
   The rocky edge under Niagara Falls has eroded <u>very</u> slowly.

8. The water is a very valuable source of electric power.
   The water is a <u>very</u> valuable source of electric power.

TRY THIS! Write a short paragraph about why you think a waterfall is a popular tourist attraction. Use adverbs in your explanation.

76 Unit 4 • Chapter 23   Practice • More About Adjectives and Adverbs

Comparing with Adjectives and Adverbs

A. Complete the sentence, using the correct form of the adjective or adverb in parentheses.

1. Rainbow Bridge in Utah is the ____largest____ natural bridge in the world. **(large)**

2. At 215 feet, Natural Bridge in West Virginia is 94 feet ____shorter____ than Rainbow Bridge. **(short)**

3. Rainbow Bridge was discovered many years ____later____ than Natural Bridge. **(late)**

4. Some natural bridges arch ____more gracefully____ than human-made bridges. **(gracefully)**

5. Natural stone bridges may erode ____more slowly____ than steel bridges. **(slowly)**

B. Choose the correct word to best complete each sentence. Then write the complete sentence.

6. This monument had the **(larger, largest)** crowd of visitors ever.
   This monument had the largest crowd of visitors ever.

7. The nights are **(colder, coldest)** than the days at this Arizona site.
   The nights are colder than the days at this Arizona site.

8. Some tour boats will leave **(earlier, earliest)** than other boats.
   Some tour boats will leave earlier than other boats.

TRY THIS! Write a few sentences about a bridge you have seen. Describe unusual features, who uses the bridge, and what the bridge crosses. Identify the adjectives and adverbs in your description.

Name _____

Special Forms

A. Complete the sentence, using the correct form of the adjective in parentheses.

1. The potholes were in ___fewer___ places this year than last. **(few)**

2. The newest roads had the ___least___ damage of all. **(little)**

3. It is ___better___ for your tires if you drive down a street without any potholes than one with many. **(good)**

4. New weatherproof roads are ___better___ than older ones. **(good)**

5. The new roads will need ___fewer___ repairs now. **(few)**

B. Complete the sentence, using the correct form of the adverb in parentheses.

6. Grass and trees can often slow down the progress of erosion ___better___ than rocks. **(well)**

7. Areas with little or no rainfall can erode ___worse___ than areas elsewhere. **(badly)**

8. The wind sculpts sand dunes ___best___ of all. **(well)**

9. Sand bounces off hard surfaces ___better___ than off soft surfaces. **(well)**

10. Ocean waves erode sandy beaches ___worst___ of all. **(badly)**

TRY THIS! Write a few sentences to explain why potholes on city streets are a problem. Use the comparative forms of the adjectives *good* and *bad* and of the adverbs *well* and *badly*.

78 Unit 4 • Chapter 23   Practice • More About Adjectives and Adverbs

Name _____

Extra Practice

A. Draw an arrow to the word that each underlined adverb modifies. Write whether that word is an adjective or an adverb.

1. Waves erode the <u>relatively</u> weak bedrock. _____adjective_____

2. Sea caves can occur <u>almost</u> anywhere. _____adverb_____

3. The caves formed by the waves are not <u>very</u> long. _____adjective_____

4. Waves pound <u>nearly</u> constantly against the rock. _____adverb_____

5. <u>Really</u> powerful jets of spray shoot into the air. _____adjective_____

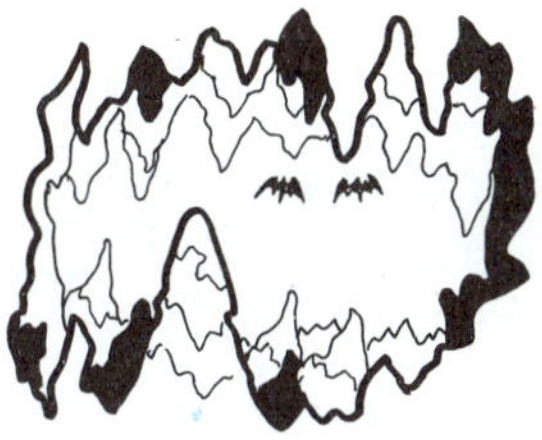

B. Write the sentence, using the correct form of the adjective or adverb in parentheses.

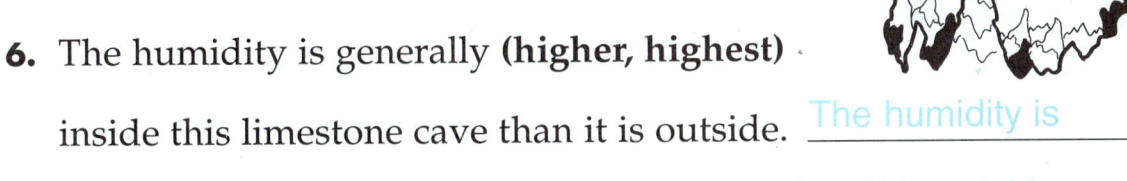

6. The humidity is generally (**higher, highest**) inside this limestone cave than it is outside. _The humidity is generally higher inside this limestone cave than it is outside._

7. The animals inside the cave live in darkness (**more, most**) easily than some other animals. _The animals inside the cave live in darkness more easily than some other animals._

8. Tours of the cave are the (**good, best**) part of the trip. _Tours of the cave are the best part of the trip._

9. Some underground lakes are (**deeper, deepest**) than others. _Some underground lakes are deeper than others._

TRY THIS! Write a paragraph about what you would expect to see in underground passages of a limestone cave. Use comparative forms of adverbs and adjectives correctly.

Practice • More About Adjectives and Adverbs

Name _____

Chapter Review

Read the passage, and choose the answer that belongs in each space. Mark the oval beside your answer.

The towns along the riverfronts were the __(1)__ towns. Riversides were the __(2)__ convenient places for homes and factories. Early settlers relied __(3)__ of all on the river for water and transportation. However, when the rivers overflowed, the __(4)__ problem of all that settlers faced was flooding. Flood control became a __(5)__ concern during heavy rains than at some other times. Some methods of flood control worked __(6)__ than others. Dams helped control most floods fairly __(7)__. Some other structures worked __(8)__ than dams.

1. ○ most early
   ○ earlier
   ● earliest
   ○ early

2. ○ more almost
   ○ almost
   ○ mostly
   ● most

3. ● most heavily
   ○ more heavily
   ○ heavier
   ○ heaviest

4. ● biggest
   ○ more big
   ○ bigger
   ○ most big

5. ○ greatly
   ● greater
   ○ greatest
   ○ great

6. ○ best
   ○ well
   ○ weller
   ● better

7. ○ good
   ○ better
   ● well
   ○ best

8. ● less smoothly
   ○ little smoothly
   ○ least smoothly
   ○ smoothly

80 Unit 4 • Chapter 23   Practice • More About Adjectives and Adverbs

Name _____

Prepositions

A. Read each sentence. Underline the preposition.

1. The subway <u>in</u> Washington, D.C., is called the Metro.
2. It stops <u>near</u> the Smithsonian museums.
3. The subway <u>between</u> San Francisco and Oakland is called BART.
4. The trains run <u>under</u> the San Francisco Bay.
5. Some BART trains run <u>above</u> the ground.

B. To complete each sentence, write a preposition from the box in the blank.

| by | from | to | over | under |

6. Lucy has rarely been very far __from__ home.
7. They are going __to__ an amusement park.
8. Lillian and her family went __by__ plane.
9. Lillian remembers flying __over__ the park and looking down.
10. Lucy is taking the submarine __under__ the water.

TRY THIS! Suppose that you are going to go to a big amusement park. Write a description of what you think it will be like and what you would like to do there. Underline the prepositions in your writing.

Practice • Prepositions   Unit 5 • Chapter 25   81

Name _____

Object of the Preposition

A. Underline the prepositional phrase in each sentence.

1. He is taking a trip to Italy and France.

2. He flies through the night.

3. Soon Mike will be in Rome, Italy.

4. They leave the airport by car.

5. The city is filled with small speeding cars and motorbikes.

B. Write each prepositional phrase. Underline the preposition once and the object of the preposition twice.

6. He sees ancient Roman buildings on a hill.
   on a hill

7. He sees modern apartments in the distance.
   in the distance

8. He walks everywhere with his friends.
   with his friends

9. They find great food in little cafés and in restaurants.
   in little cafés   in restaurants

10. Mike plays soccer with some Italian children.
    with some Italian children

TRY THIS! Write an advertisement to get people to come to live in your city. Include several prepositional phrases in your writing, and underline them.

82   Unit 5 • Chapter 25   Practice • Prepositions

Name _____

Using Prepositional Phrases

A. Expand each sentence. Add a prepositional phrase. Use the preposition in parentheses. *Possible responses are shown.*

1. Barbara likes going _____ to concerts _____ . **(to)**
2. She can travel easily _____ on buses _____ . **(on)**
3. Barbara enjoys listening _____ to pop and classical music _____ . **(to)**
4. Robert spends time _____ at the history museum _____ . **(at)**
5. He likes looking _____ at old cars and armor _____ . **(at)**

B. Write each sentence. Add details with one or more prepositional phrases. Underline each preposition. *Possible responses are shown.*

6. Sue is going.
   Sue is going <u>to</u> a café <u>for</u> lunch.

7. She and her mother will eat.
   She and her mother will eat <u>at</u> noon.

8. Finally they arrive.
   Finally they arrive <u>at</u> the restaurant.

9. They order their food.
   They order their food <u>from</u> the waiter.

10. Their food is served.
    Their food is served <u>after</u> ten minutes.

TRY THIS! Write a description of a recent experience at a restaurant. Include at least three prepositional phrases in your writing, and underline them.

Practice • Prepositions Unit 5 • Chapter 25 83

Name _____

Extra Practice

A. Read each sentence. Underline the preposition once and underline the object of the preposition twice.

1. It is very hot there <u>during</u> the <u>summer</u>.

2. At <u>night</u>, sleeping can be difficult.

3. It can be hot <u>in</u> <u>winter</u> too.

4. There are mountains <u>near</u> <u>Tucson</u>.

5. Sometimes it snows <u>in</u> the <u>mountains</u>.

B. Add a prepositional phrase to each sentence. Then write the new sentence. *Possible responses are shown.*

6. Some of them leave.

   Some of them leave in cars.

7. Others take trains.

   Others take trains from the city.

8. Some people would rather stay.

   Some people would rather stay in the city.

9. Richard enjoys city activities.

   Richard enjoys city activities with his friends.

10. He has not been to the circus.

    He has not been to the circus since last year.

TRY THIS! Write a paragraph that compares the different ways people can travel in cities. Describe some of the good points and the bad points of each way of traveling.

Name _____

Chapter Review

Read the passage. Choose the term that names the underlined word or words. Mark the oval beside your answer.

Maria and her family live **(1)** in Sacramento, California. There are many interesting things to see and do **(2)** near her house. Maria likes to walk around **(3)** Old Town. There is a museum where you can learn **(4)** about trains and railroads. Maria also enjoys going into **(5)** the old one-room schoolhouse. She likes to walk **(6)** by the river. She watches the boats on **(7)** the water.

1. ○ Preposition
   ○ Object of the preposition
   ○ Prepositional phrase
   ○ Word between the preposition and the object of the preposition

2. ○ Preposition
   ○ Object of the preposition
   ● Prepositional phrase
   ○ Words between the preposition and the object of the preposition

3. ○ Preposition
   ● Object of the preposition
   ○ Prepositional phrase
   ○ Words between the preposition and the object of the preposition

4. ○ Preposition
   ○ Object of the preposition
   ● Prepositional phrase
   ○ Words between the preposition and the object of the preposition

5. ○ Preposition
   ○ Object of the preposition
   ○ Prepositional phrase
   ● Word between the preposition and the object of the preposition

6. ○ Preposition
   ○ Object of the preposition
   ● Prepositional phrase
   ○ Words between the preposition and the object of the preposition

7. ○ Preposition
   ○ Object of the preposition
   ○ Prepositional phrase
   ● Word between the preposition and the object of the preposition

Practice • Prepositions

Name _____

Independent Clauses

A. Write whether each group of words is a phrase or an independent clause.

1. the Northwest can be very damp   _independent clause_

2. wet and rainy in the winter   _phrase_

3. the rain forests in the Olympic Mountains   _phrase_

4. huge ferns and dense green forests   _phrase_

5. the rainfall is heavy each year   _independent clause_

B. Write whether each group of words is a phrase or an independent clause. Write each independent clause. Capitalize and punctuate it correctly.

6. it seems as though it never stops raining

   independent clause; It seems as though it never stops raining.

7. very different in the Southwest

   phrase

8. there is very little rain in the Southwest

   independent clause; There is very little rain in the Southwest.

9. months without rain in some places

   phrase

TRY THIS! Write a journal entry that describes your travels in a hot and dry place. Explain where you are, what you are doing, and what you see. Circle the phrases, and underline the clauses.

86   Unit 5 • Chapter 26   Practice • Phrases and Clauses

Name _____

Dependent Clauses

A. Underline the dependent clause in each sentence.

1. There are many old houses in New England <u>because they were built to last</u>.

2. <u>Although some houses may be big</u>, the ceilings are often low.

3. Builders also used stone, <u>which they found almost everywhere</u>.

4. <u>When you go to New England</u>, you will see many stone walls.

5. People used stones <u>when they built chimneys</u>.

B. Write the dependent clause in each sentence. Then circle the connecting word that begins the clause.

6. Because the ponds freeze in winter, many people go ice-skating.
   (Because) the ponds freeze in winter

7. Some people fish in winter after they have made a hole in the ice.
   (after) they have made a hole in the ice

8. When it is warm, people swim in the ponds.
   (When) it is warm

9. People can dive into many ponds unless the water is shallow.
   (unless) the water is shallow

10. Always inquire whether diving is allowed and safe.
    (whether) diving is allowed and safe

TRY THIS! Write a paragraph about a body of water near your home. Describe what happens there in the winter and in the summer. Include dependent clauses in your writing.

Practice • Phrases and Clauses   Unit 5 • Chapter 26   87

Name _____

Distinguishing Independent and Dependent Clauses

A. Read each sentence. Underline the independent clause once and the dependent clause twice. Circle the connecting word.

1. Amy goes to the Delaware shore (where) her family spends the summer.
2. She gets up very early (because) so many birds are out at that time.
3. (While) she is looking for birds, she also picks up special shells.
4. (When) she walks near the ocean, tiny crabs move across the sand.
5. Often she is out (before) the sun comes up.

B. Label each clause *independent* or *dependent*.

6. The waves break on the shore. _____independent_____
7. The sunrise is very beautiful. _____independent_____
8. Because it rises right over the ocean. _____dependent_____
9. After the last big storm was over. _____dependent_____
10. All kinds of great things washed up onto the beach. _____independent_____

TRY THIS! Suppose that you are spending several weeks at a beach. Write a letter to a friend telling about some of your adventures. Use dependent clauses correctly in your writing.

88   Unit 5 • Chapter 26   Practice • Phrases and Clauses

Name _____

Extra Practice

A. Write whether each group of words is a phrase or an independent clause. If the group of words is an independent clause, underline the complete subject once and the complete predicate twice.

1. Will fly into Cincinnati today. _____phrase_____

2. <u>The city</u> <u><u>has a large river nearby</u></u>. _____independent clause_____

3. Boats on the river. _____phrase_____

4. <u>The river</u> <u><u>is called the Ohio River</u></u>. _____independent clause_____

5. Outside of the city. _____phrase_____

B. Read each sentence. Underline the independent clause once and the dependent clause twice.

6. <u><u>While there are many things to do in Cincinnati,</u></u> <u>walking in a nearby forest is fun.</u>

7. <u>You could also go for a boat ride on the river</u> <u><u>when the weather is good.</u></u>

8. <u><u>If you cross the river,</u></u> <u>you will be in another state.</u>

9. <u>You will enter Kentucky,</u> <u><u>where some people raise horses.</u></u>

10. <u>Kentucky is a state</u> <u><u>where many people work in coal mines.</u></u>

11. <u><u>When winter comes,</u></u> <u>coal is used for heat.</u>

12. <u>The state's nickname is the *Bluegrass State*</u> <u><u>because a certain grass with a bluish-green color grows there.</u></u>

TRY THIS! Write some directions for how to get to a vacation spot near where you live. Tell the name of the place, and describe the kind of place it is. Include independent and dependent clauses.

Practice • Phrases and Clauses   Unit 5 • Chapter 26   89

Name _____

Chapter Review

Look for mistakes in the use of independent and dependent clauses in the sentences below. Choose the best way to write each sentence, and fill in the oval for your answer. If the sentence has no mistake, fill in the oval beside *No mistake*.

1. Hurricanes sometimes hit the Gulf, and cause problems.
   - ○ Hurricanes sometimes hit the Gulf and, cause problems.
   - ⬤ Hurricanes sometimes hit the Gulf and cause problems.
   - ○ Sometimes hit the Gulf and cause problems.
   - ○ No mistake

2. Hurricane winds can cause damage. When they hit.
   - ○ Hurricane winds can cause damage when. They hit.
   - ⬤ Hurricane winds can cause damage when they hit.
   - ○ Hurricane winds can cause damage when, they hit.
   - ○ No mistake

3. Along the coast, high tides and storms can cause large floods.
   - ○ Along the coast high tides, and storms can cause large floods
   - ○ Along the coast high tides and storms. Can cause large floods.
   - ○ Along the coast, high tides and storms. Can cause large floods.
   - ⬤ No mistake

4. Trees bend, when the wind reaches 100 miles per hour.
   - ⬤ Trees bend when the wind reaches 100 miles per hour.
   - ○ Trees bend, When the wind reaches 100 miles per hour.
   - ○ Trees bend. When the wind reaches 100 miles per hour.
   - ○ No mistake

5. Boats are destroyed. Before they can reach shore.
   - ○ Boats are destroyed, Before they can reach shore.
   - ⬤ Boats are destroyed before they can reach shore.
   - ○ Boats are destroyed before, they can reach shore.
   - ○ No mistake

6. People protect windows. From high winds with plywood.
   - ○ People protect windows, from high winds with plywood.
   - ⬤ People protect windows from high winds with plywood.
   - ○ People protect windows from high winds, with plywood.
   - ○ No mistake

90   Unit 5 • Chapter 26   Practice • Phrases and Clauses

Name _____

Complex Sentences

A. Write whether or not each sentence is a complex sentence.

1. Several different crops are grown on a mixed farm. _____not complex_____

2. Wheat, corn, and soybeans were grown on the mixed farm. _____not complex_____

3. Corn is grown as a cereal grain. _____complex_____

4. When the demand for milk increased, dairy farmers bought more dairy cows. _____complex_____

5. When more than half a farm is used to grow one crop, the farm is a specialized farm. _____complex_____

B. Underline the independent clause once and the dependent clause twice in each complex sentence. If the sentence is not complex, write *not complex*.

6. Most plants grow best when they are irrigated with fresh water. _____

7. Sometimes irrigation water comes from lakes. _____not complex_____

8. The fresh lake water is used to help crops grow. _____not complex_____

9. When the river water rises, the dam holds it back. _____

10. When a dam is built, a large lake forms. _____

TRY THIS! Write a paragraph describing a lake, a river, or an ocean in your area. Use complex sentences in your writing.

Practice • Complex Sentences   Unit 5 • Chapter 28   91

Name _____

More About Complex Sentences

A. Fill in the blank with a word from the box that completes each sentence. You may use a word more than once.

though   before   after   when   because   where

1. Animals can drink fresh water ____after____ it rains.

2. ____Before____ people can use the river water for drinking, it must be cleaned.

3. ____When____ you are thirsty, you drink water.

4. ____Because____ the river is nearby, it is the city's water source.

5. Many large cities were built ____where____ there was a lot of water people could use.

B. Underline the dependent clause in each sentence.

6. Ships travel between cities <u>when rivers are wide enough</u>.

7. A harbor is a place <u>where ships dock</u>.

8. <u>Before it leaves the harbor</u>, a ship is loaded with goods.

9. The goods are unloaded <u>when the ship reaches a harbor in another city</u>.

10. <u>If a city has a harbor</u>, there are many jobs for people there.

11. Goods <u>that come into a country</u> are imports.

12. <u>After a ship is loaded with goods</u>, it takes the goods, or exports, to another country.

TRY THIS! Write a short paragraph about a trip you might take on a river. What would you see? Use complex sentences in your writing.

92   Unit 5 • Chapter 28   Practice • Complex Sentences

Name _____

Commas in Complex Sentences

A. Add a comma to the sentence where it is needed. If a sentence does not need a comma, write *No comma*.

1. A national park is a valuable area because it is kept in its natural state. _____No comma_____

2. Before 1872 there were no national parks in the United States. _____

3. Yellowstone was the first national park. _____No comma_____

4. Since Yellowstone National Park opened, millions of people have visited it. _____

5. When you visit, you must obey the rules. _____

B. Write each sentence, placing a comma where needed. If a sentence needs no comma, write *No comma*. If a sentence is complex, write *Complex*.

6. Some sports are not allowed because they may damage national parks. _No comma; Complex_

7. Although people can ski in some national parks they must stay on ski trails. _Although people can ski in some national parks, they must stay on ski trails. Complex_

8. Since the giant redwood trees in Redwood National Park are valuable the park protects them. _Since the giant redwood trees in Redwood National Park are valuable, the park protects them. Complex_

TRY THIS! Write a short description of an interesting place to visit in your state. Use complex sentences in your writing.

Practice • Complex Sentences

Name _____

Extra Practice

A. Write whether or not each sentence is a complex sentence.

1. Farmers in ancient Egypt raised sheep, goats, and pigs. _____ not complex _____

2. They grew cotton because they could weave it into cloth. _____ complex _____

3. Barley became an important crop as the Egyptians learned to farm. _____ complex _____

4. Towns were built in areas where farmers grew food. _____ complex _____

5. The best farms were along the Nile River where the soil was rich. _____ complex _____

B. If a sentence needs a comma, write the sentence correctly. If a sentence does not need a comma, write *No comma*.

6. A plow digs up the soil as it moves.
   No comma

7. Because old plows were so heavy they were pulled by strong work animals. Because old plows were so heavy, they were pulled by strong work animals.

8. The plow that farmers use today is like the one used years ago.
   No comma

9. When a farmer today uses a plow it is powered by an engine.
   When a farmer today uses a plow, it is powered by an engine.

TRY THIS! Write a few sentences about an invention you think is very important today. Use complex sentences in your writing.

Name _____

Chapter Review

Read the passage, and choose the answer that belongs in each numbered space below. Fill in the oval next to your choice.

__(1)__ people in ancient times learned to plant and harvest, farming has been important in Egypt. In ancient Egypt, __(2)__ nearly all people worked the land, they did not own their farms. The farmers rented the land __(3)__ they farmed it. __(4)__ the crops were gathered, farmers gave part of the crop to the landowner. Farmers paid the landowner for every acre of land they farmed. Unless the farmers paid the rent __(5)__ could not farm the land. __(6)__ they were ready to plant __(7)__ farmers got seed from the landowners. __(8)__ landowners controlled everything on the farm, they did not work as farmers.

1. ○ Before
   ○ If
   ● Ever since
   ○ Although

2. ○ since
   ○ after
   ● although
   ○ , where

3. ● before
   ○ , except
   ○ except
   ○ , that

4. ○ Which,
   ○ Since
   ○ Still,
   ● After

5. ○ who,
   ● , they
   ○ they,
   ○ that

6. ○ Which
   ● When
   ○ Who
   ○ Which,

7. ● crops,
   ○ crops
   ○ crops.
   ○ crops?

8. ○ Before
   ○ Or
   ○ That,
   ● Although

Practice • Complex Sentences   Unit 5 • Chapter 28   95

Name _____

Sentence Fragments

A. Write whether each group of words is a sentence fragment or a complete sentence.

1. The sea is deep and wide. _____ complete sentence _____

2. The rapids and the currents near the shore. _____ sentence fragment _____

3. The rain forest surrounds the river for its entire length. _____ complete sentence _____

4. A hot, wet climate. _____ sentence fragment _____

5. Green and twisted vines hanging from the trees. _____ sentence fragment _____

B. Write whether each of the following groups of words is a complete sentence or a sentence fragment. If an item is a sentence fragment, write whether it is missing a subject, predicate, or both.

6. Suns himself on the banks. _____ sentence fragment; no subject _____

7. Old and famous legends of the Amazon. _____ sentence fragment; no predicate _____

8. We will visit the Amazon delta. _____ complete sentence _____

9. Flocks of wild birds fish in the river. _____ complete sentence _____

10. Sunlight through the trees. _____ sentence fragment; no predicate _____

11. Was sparkling on the water. _____ sentence fragment; no subject _____

TRY THIS! Write a description of a river or a stream you have visited. Underline the subject and the verb in each sentence to make sure that you have no sentence fragments.

Name _____

Run-On Sentences

A. Write each run-on sentence as two separate sentences.

1. The desert is dry its soil is poor.

   The desert is dry. Its soil is poor.

2. Trees cannot live in the dunes they live by the river.

   Trees cannot live in the dunes. They live by the river.

3. Palm trees give us dates they provide shade.

   Palm trees give us dates. They provide shade.

4. Crops need water they will die without it.

   Crops need water. They will die without it.

5. In the wet season the rain falls the river rises quickly.

   In the wet season the rain falls. The river rises quickly.

B. Write each run-on sentence correctly. Add a comma and a conjunction to join two complete thoughts. Use the conjunction *and, or,* or *but*.
Possible responses are shown.

6. Visit the Nile you will see many farms.

   Visit the Nile, and you will see many farms.

7. You may see camels you may see cars and buses.

   You may see camels, or you may see cars and buses.

8. The Nile Delta is open land it is often marshy.

   The Nile Delta is open land, and it is often marshy.

TRY THIS! Suppose you are writing for a travel magazine. Write a brief story about a visit to the Nile River. Make sure that you have no run-on sentences.

Practice • Sentence Fragments and Run-On Sentences

Name _____

Correcting Sentence Errors

A. Proofread each run-on sentence. Add punctuation and capitalize as needed.

1. It is far in the north. It is near the northern part of Russia.

2. Summer days are long. The sun shines many hours.

3. People fish the delta. They work long days.

4. The Russian sun is bright. The Russian sun sparkles on the water.

5. This is a good day. A good day brings many fish.

B. Correct each run-on sentence by adding a comma and the conjunction given in parentheses.

6. Some people fish with lines they use nets. **(or)**
   Some people fish with lines, or they use nets.

7. Fish are hauled into the boat they are sorted. **(and)**
   Fish are hauled into the boat, and they are sorted.

8. Caviar is taken from sturgeon salt is added. **(and)**
   Caviar is taken from sturgeon, and salt is added.

9. Russian caviar is the best kind it is prized in other countries. **(and)**
   Russian caviar is the best kind, and it is prized in other countries.

10. Do you like caviar do you prefer anchovies? **(or)**
    Do you like caviar, or do you prefer anchovies?

TRY THIS! Write five sentences about how people use rivers. Avoid run-on sentences and sentence fragments.

Name _____

Extra Practice

A. Write whether each group of words is a sentence fragment or a complete sentence.

1. Settled near rivers and used the water. _____sentence fragment_____

2. There were no cars, but boats were good transportation. _____complete sentence_____

3. Busy ports along the river. _____sentence fragment_____

4. Merchants traded goods and shopped in town. _____complete sentence_____

5. Ships still carry freight to city ports. _____complete sentence_____

B. Correct each run-on sentence by adding a comma and a conjunction to create a complete sentence.

6. Boats travel the Amazon there is much river traffic.
   Boats travel the Amazon, and there is much river traffic.

7. Streams from high in the mountains become rivers they flow to the ocean. Streams from high in the mountains become rivers, and they flow to the ocean.

8. There are many towns beside the rivers not all towns have ports.
   There are many towns beside the rivers, but not all towns have ports.

9. Rivers collect more water they grow deeper and wider.
   Rivers collect more water, and they grow deeper and wider.

TRY THIS! Write a poem about the sounds of a river. When you have finished writing, underline and correct sentence fragments.

Practice • Sentence Fragments and Run-On Sentences

Name _____

Chapter Review

Read the passage. Some sections are underlined. Choose the best way to write each underlined section, and fill in the oval for your choice. If the underlined section needs no change, choose *No mistake*.

(1) The river in our town is a beautiful place. (2) We picnic on the grass we watch boats travel along. The river is wide and green. (3) Sometimes a tugboat pulls a barge up the river. It chugs slowly by our park. (4) Sometimes a pleasure boat full of music and people. People fish from the pier. (5) Plentiful trout. (6) Farther downstream the children play in the water you can hear them laughing. (7) My brother swims I float on my raft. (8) Reads a book.

1. ○ Sentence fragment—no subject
   ○ Sentence fragment—no predicate
   ○ Run-on sentence
   ● No mistake

2. ○ Sentence fragment—no subject
   ○ Sentence fragment—no predicate
   ● Run-on sentence
   ○ No mistake

3. ○ Sentence fragment—no subject
   ○ Sentence fragment—no predicate
   ○ Run-on sentence
   ● No mistake

4. ○ Sentence fragment—no subject
   ● Sentence fragment—no predicate
   ○ Run-on sentence
   ○ No mistake

5. ○ Sentence fragment—no subject
   ● Sentence fragment—no predicate
   ○ Run-on sentence
   ○ No mistake

6. ○ Sentence fragment—no subject
   ○ Sentence fragment—no predicate
   ● Run-on sentence
   ○ No mistake

7. ○ Sentence fragment—no subject
   ○ Sentence fragment—no predicate
   ● Run-on sentence
   ○ No mistake

8. ● Sentence fragment—no subject
   ○ Sentence fragment—no predicate
   ○ Run-on sentence
   ○ No mistake

Commas

A. Proofread the sentence. Add a comma where it is needed. A sentence may need more than one comma.

1. Tara, will you help set up the tent?

2. Yes, I remember that the tent stakes should be hammered into the ground.

3. The stars, the moon, and flashlights are our only lights at night.

4. Lola, our favorite camp counselor, showed us how to complete the ropes course.

5. When it is snowing, I sigh, smile, and remember summer camp.

B. Write the sentence. Add a comma where it is needed. A sentence may need more than one comma.

6. Of course we learned to paddle a canoe.
   Of course, we learned to paddle a canoe.

7. Sammie Tara's little sister stayed in a tent with the youngest kids.
   Sammie, Tara's little sister, stayed in a tent with the youngest kids.

8. Tara and I both experienced campers helped build the bonfire.
   Tara and I, both experienced campers, helped build the bonfire.

TRY THIS! Write a brief story about an afternoon on a lake. Tell about two characters who have fun swimming, rafting, or canoeing. Place commas where they are needed.

Practice • Commas and Colons   Unit 6 • Chapter 31   101

Name _____

Colons

A. Write each sentence. Add a colon where needed.

1. The buffet offered the following choices eggs, cereal, and toast.
   The buffet offered the following choices: eggs, cereal, and toast.

2. I wrote postcards to these friends Ruben, Hillary, and Asia.
   I wrote postcards to these friends: Ruben, Hillary, and Asia.

3. At 900 everyone gathered for a hike.
   At 9:00 everyone gathered for a hike.

4. We reached the summit of Mt. Osborne before 100.
   We reached the summit of Mt. Osborne before 1:00.

B. If the sentence needs a colon, write the sentence and add a colon. Write *Correct* if the sentence is correct.

5. At 900 at night, the campers went to their tents.
   At 9:00 at night, the campers went to their tents.

6. I made these new friends at camp Maria, Jasmine, and Rudy.
   I made these new friends at camp: Maria, Jasmine, and Rudy.

7. I enjoy these days and nights at camp.
   Correct

8. We have the following activities woodcraft, swimming, and singing.
   We have the following activities: woodcraft, swimming, and singing.

TRY THIS! Write a recipe for a great campsite meal. List the ingredients, and tell what time the meal will be served. Include three sentences that require colons.

102 Unit 6 • Chapter 31   Practice • Commas and Colons

Commas Versus Colons

A. Write the numbers or words. Add a comma or a colon where needed.

1. 1030 — 10:30
2. Dear Senator Little — Dear Senator Little:
3. Sincerely — Sincerely,
4. May 20 2002 — May 20, 2002
5. Denver Colorado — Denver, Colorado

B. Write the letter, adding commas and colons where needed. A sentence may need more than one comma.

(6) Dear Grandma
   (7) Well I am writing from summer camp. (8) We have these new activities a ropes course, sailing lessons, and outdoor gymnastics. (9) I have been staying up until 900 every night.
                      (10) Love
                        Margaret

(6) Dear Grandma,

   (7) Well, I am writing from summer camp. (8) We have these new activities: a ropes course, sailing lessons, and outdoor gymnastics. (9) I have been staying up until 9:00 every night.

                      (10) Love,
                        Margaret

TRY THIS! Write a letter to a friend. Tell about a national, state, or local park. Place commas correctly. Include at least one colon that comes before a list.

Practice • Commas and Colons

Name _____

Extra Practice

A. Write the numbers or words. Add a comma or a colon where needed.

1. Clear Lake California — Clear Lake, California
2. 530 tonight — 5:30 tonight
3. Dear Tara — Dear Tara,
4. Well hello! — Well, hello!
5. Dear Mrs. Goodman — Dear Mrs. Goodman:

B. Write the letter below. Correct all errors.

(6) Dear Aunt Sally
  Are you going to Lake Arrowhead next week? (7) Well: we are! (8) I have a new canoe a green Pioneer. (9) Randall taught me the following boating rules: never stand up, steer from the back, and center your weight. (10) Meet us by the lifeguard stand at 100!
    Love,
    Tara

(6) Dear Aunt Sally,

  Are you going to Lake Arrowhead next week? (7) Well, we are!

(8) I have a new canoe, a green Pioneer. (9) Randall taught me

the following boating rules: never stand up, steer from the back, and

center your weight. (10) Meet us by the lifeguard stand at 1:00!

    Love,

    Tara

TRY THIS! Write a letter from Tara to you. Have her tell about an adventure in her canoe. Use commas and colons correctly.

104 Unit 6 • Chapter 31   Practice • Commas and Colons

Name _____

Chapter Review

Look for a mistake in punctuation in each sentence below. Choose the best way to write each sentence and fill in the oval for your answer. If the sentence has no mistake, fill in the oval for the choice *No mistake*.

1 Please, when you get up at 6:00, do not wake the other campers!
- ◯ Please when you get up at 6:00, do not wake the other campers!
- ◯ Please, when you get up at 600, do not wake the other campers!
- ◯ Please when you get up at 600, do not wake the other campers!
- ⬤ No mistake

2 Leave the campground clean, taking only the following things memories, photographs, and friends.
- ◯ Leave the campground clean, taking only the following things, memories, photographs, and friends.
- ⬤ Leave the campground clean, taking only the following things: memories, photographs, and friends.
- ◯ Leave the campground clean, taking only the following things: memories photographs and friends.
- ◯ No mistake

3 Mr. Ramirez José's uncle will teach us how to tie knots.
- ⬤ Mr. Ramirez, José's uncle, will teach us how to tie knots.
- ◯ Mr. Ramirez: José's uncle will teach us how to tie knots.
- ◯ Mr. Ramirez José's uncle, will teach us how to tie knots.
- ◯ No mistake

4 On December 12 2001 the camping club will meet at 3:00.
- ⬤ On December 12, 2001, the camping club will meet at 3:00.
- ◯ On December 12, 2001, the camping club will meet at 300.
- ◯ On December 12 2001, the camping club will meet at 3:00.
- ◯ No mistake

Practice • Commas and Colons

Unit 6 • Chapter 31   105

Name _____

Underlining and Using Quotation Marks in Titles

A. Write the title in each sentence correctly.

1. Joseph's band plays songs such as The Train. ——— "The Train"

2. They play another song called Take Me There. ——— "Take Me There"

3. Sometimes they learn songs from the book 100 Best Songs. ——— 100 Best Songs

4. They use another book called 1990s Songs. ——— 1990s Songs

5. Joseph wrote a song called The Ferris Wheel. ——— "The Ferris Wheel"

B. Use underlines or quotation marks to write each title correctly.

6. Twenty Years at Sea **(book)** ——— Twenty Years at Sea

7. The Cloudy Day **(poem)** ——— "The Cloudy Day"

8. Independent News **(newspaper)** ——— Independent News

9. Guitar **(magazine)** ——— Guitar

10. The Mouse and the Cat **(story)** ——— "The Mouse and the Cat"

TRY THIS! Write a few sentences that tell about two of your favorite songs. Write the title of each song correctly.

106 Unit 6 • Chapter 32   Practice • Titles and Quotation Marks

Name _____

Capitalizing Words in Titles

A. Write the sentence, punctuating each title correctly.

1. Donny reads about pottery in blue rock times.
   Donny reads about pottery in Blue Rock Times.

2. He learned to make a bowl from an article in pottery magazine.
   He learned to make a bowl from an article in Pottery Magazine.

3. Donny wrote a story about a potter called "where's my wheel?"
   Donny wrote a story about a potter called "Where's My Wheel?"

4. His sister, Linda, writes poems such as "stay out of my room!"
   His sister, Linda, writes poems such as "Stay Out of My Room!"

5. Her favorite poetry book is called poetry for all ages.
   Her favorite poetry book is called Poetry for All Ages.

B. Write each title correctly.

6. The pearl (book) — The Pearl

7. if (poem) — "If"

8. "the new kids are here" (magazine article) — "The New Kids Are Here"

9. kid's Week (magazine) — Kid's Week

10. bayside gazette (newspaper) — Bayside Gazette

TRY THIS! Write a paragraph that tells about magazines you like to read. Tell what each magazine is about and name some articles you have read. Be sure to write the magazine and article titles correctly.

Practice • Titles and Quotation Marks   Unit 6 • Chapter 32   107

Name _____

Hyphens

A. Write the hyphenated word in each sentence. Tell why the word is hyphenated.

1. I read twenty-two books this summer.
   twenty-two; compound word

2. The last one I read had an unusual yellow-orange cover.
   yellow-orange; compound word

3. Some of the stories were long and I had trouble under-standing them. understanding; end of line

4. I had to reach for the tip-top shelf to get one book.
   tip-top; compound word

5. No one expected me to read more books than the librar-ian. librarian; end of line

B. Each phrase contains a compound word that should be hyphenated. Write each compound word correctly.

6. a well read magazine — well-read
7. a small town newspaper — small-town
8. a 105 year old man — 105-year-old
9. add on decals — add-on
10. a dark, blue gray color — a dark, blue-gray

TRY THIS! Suppose you must write a book review for a newspaper. Write the name of the newspaper you are writing for, the title of the article you are writing, and the title of the book you are reviewing.

108 Unit 6 • Chapter 32   Practice • Titles and Quotation Marks

Name _____

Extra Practice

A. Write each sentence. Underline or put quotation marks around each title.

1. People from Forty Countries is a story in the book he read.
   "People from Forty Countries" is a story in the book he read.

2. Lee builds the models that he sees in Model Magazine.
   Lee builds the models that he sees in <u>Model Magazine</u>.

3. He finds ideas for models in the Lincoln Gazette newspaper.
   He finds ideas for models in the <u>Lincoln Gazette</u> newspaper.

4. He found a library book called 101 Models You Can Make.
   He found a library book called <u>101 Models You Can Make</u>.

5. Lee found another book called How to Make Model Airplanes.
   Lee found another book called <u>How to Make Model Airplanes</u>.

B. Each title contains one or more errors. Use correct capitalization, underlining, and quotation marks to write each title correctly.

6. "Healthful recipes For Your Family"   **(book)**
   <u>Healthful Recipes for Your Family</u>

7. Games and hobbies   **(book)**   <u>Games and Hobbies</u>

8. "Sue diamond and The amazing Butterflies"   **(story)**
   "Sue Diamond and the Amazing Butterflies"

9. Stories for kids   **(magazine)**   <u>Stories for Kids</u>

TRY THIS! Suppose that you are working in a library. Write the titles of four books, three stories, and two magazines to recommend for people your age. Write each title correctly.

Practice • Titles and Quotation Marks

Unit 6 • Chapter 32   109

Name _____

Chapter Review

Look for a mistake in punctuation in each sentence below. Choose the correct way to write each sentence, and fill in the oval next to your answer. If the sentence has no mistake, choose *No mistake*.

1 Jeff's favorite book is The Best Band on Ice.

○ Jeff's favorite book is "The Best Band on Ice."
○ Jeff's favorite book is "The Best Band on Ice."
○ Jeff's favorite book is The Best Band on Ice.
● No mistake

2 Jeff's band plays "The Three Step March."

○ Jeff's band plays "The Three-Step-March."
○ Jeff's band plays "The Three Step-March."
● Jeff's band plays "The Three-Step March."
○ No mistake

3 The band learns songs from the book "My Favorite Marches."

○ The band learns songs from the book "My favorite Marches."
○ The band learns songs from the book My favorite Marches.
● The band learns songs from the book My Favorite Marches.
○ No mistake

4 Jeff's great uncle gave him a second-hand trumpet.

● Jeff's great-uncle gave him a secondhand trumpet.
○ Jeff's great uncle gave him a second hand trumpet.
○ Jeff's greatuncle gave him a secondhand trumpet.
○ No mistake

5 Jeff wears his great-grandfather's team-jersey.

○ Jeff wears his great grand-father's team jersey.
● Jeff wears his great-grandfather's team jersey.
○ Jeff wears his great grandfather's team jersey.
○ No mistake

6 Jeff wrote a story about him called "a Day for heroes."

● Jeff wrote a story about him called "A Day for Heroes."
○ Jeff wrote a story about him called "A Day For Heroes."
○ Jeff wrote a story about him called "A Day for heroes."
○ No mistake

110   Unit 6 • Chapter 32   Practice • Titles and Quotation Marks

Name _____

Quotation Marks in Direct Quotations

A. Underline the direct quotation from each sentence.

1. Sara said, "<u>I play on a Little League team now.</u>"

2. She added, "<u>I played Tee Ball when I was six.</u>"

3. "<u>We hit the ball off a tee,</u>" she explained.

4. She continued, "<u>The next year we played with pitching machines.</u>"

5. "<u>Have you ever tried pitching?</u>" Josh asked.

B. Write each sentence correctly. Add quotation marks and capital letters.

6. I play for the Cardinals, said Andy.
   "I play for the Cardinals," said Andy.

7. What position do you play? Josh asked.
   "What position do you play?" Josh asked.

8. I play catcher, replied Andy.
   "I play catcher," replied Andy.

9. Josh, what sport do you play? asked Andy.
   "Josh, what sport do you play?" asked Andy.

10. Josh said, well, I guess basketball is my favorite game.
    Josh said, "Well, I guess basketball is my favorite game."

11. I like basketball, too, Andy said.
    "I like basketball, too," Andy said.

TRY THIS! Write a dialogue between two of your favorite sports stars. Write at least six sentences that contain direct quotations.

Practice • More About Quotation Marks   Unit 6 • Chapter 34   111

Name _____

Quotation Marks with Dialogue

A. Identify where to begin a new paragraph. Write *Correct* if no new paragraph is needed.

(1) Hannah said, "My softball team plays every weekend."

Sam walked over to talk with the girls. "I saw your game the other day," he said. **(2)** "It was so exciting!"

Hannah said, "Coach let Lauren pitch, and she did a great job." **(3)** "What is the difference between softball and baseball?" asked Sam.

(4) "Well," said Hannah, "the ball is bigger and softer in softball."

1. Correct because Hannah is speaking
2. Correct because Sam is still speaking
3. New paragraph because Sam is a new speaker
4. Correct because Hannah is a new speaker

B. Write each direct quotation in a sentence that tells how the speaker given in parentheses said it.
Possible responses are shown.

5. Softball is so exciting! How do I sign up?   **(Megan)**
   "Softball is so exciting!" said Megan. "How do I sign up?"

6. I'll tell my coach to call you.   **(Hannah)**
   "I'll tell my coach to call you," answered Hannah.

7. I have never hit a softball before.   **(Megan)**
   "I have never hit a softball before," said Megan.

TRY THIS!   Suppose that Megan has joined the team and is playing center field. Write a conversation that Hannah and Megan might have during a game. Write at least six direct quotations in your dialogue.

112   Unit 6 • Chapter 34   Practice • More About Quotation Marks

Punctuating Dialogue

A. Write *Correct* if the sentence is punctuated correctly. If the punctuation is not correct, write the sentence correctly.

1. Charles asked "How is your team doing?"
   Charles asked, "How is your team doing?"

2. "We win about half the games." answered Roberto.
   "We win about half the games," answered Roberto.

3. He went on, "Mostly, we just play for fun."
   Correct

4. "My father says it is how you play that counts," he added.
   Correct

5. "And, you know" he said, "it's fun to work with the team."
   "And, you know," he said, "it's fun to work with the team."

B. Write each sentence correctly by adding punctuation.

6. "In basketball," Roberto explained "the players run all the time.
   "In basketball," Roberto explained, "the players run all the time."

7. He added Running is good for your heart."
   He added, "Running is good for your heart."

8. "Besides" he continued Coach wants us to warm up.
   "Besides," he continued, "Coach wants us to warm up."

TRY THIS! Write a dialogue between a coach and members of a sports team. Include six direct quotations in your dialogue. Use interrogative, exclamatory, imperative, and declarative sentences.

Practice • More About Quotation Marks   Unit 6 • Chapter 34

Name _____

Extra Practice

A. Write each sentence correctly. Add punctuation where it is needed.

   1. Students should run and play every day. Mrs. McMann said

      "Students should run and play every day," Mrs. McMann said.

   2. Breathing hard is good for your lungs she explained.

      "Breathing hard is good for your lungs," she explained.

   3. Kim said I take ballet lessons at the community center.

      Kim said, "I take ballet lessons at the community center."

   4. Mrs. McMann said People should get exercise all their lives.

      Mrs. McMann said, "People should get exercise all their lives."

B. Each underlined item has at least one error. Explain how each item can be written correctly.

   Mrs. McMann looked at her students. "What other kinds of exercise are there?" she asked. **(5)** <u>Kim said "My mother goes to a gym. She is strong and healthy."</u> **(6)** <u>"I like skiing." said Carol, "and sledding, too."</u>
   Mrs. McMann continued the discussion. **(7)** <u>"It is important to eat right, too." she said.</u>

   5. Begin a new paragraph; add a comma after *said*.

   6. Begin a new paragraph. Replace the first period with a comma.

   7. Replace the first period with a comma.

TRY THIS! Work with a partner to write more dialogue about how to stay healthy. Write at least six direct quotations.

114 Unit 6 • Chapter 34   Practice • More About Quotation Marks

Name _____

Chapter Review

Decide which type of mistake, if any, appears in each underlined section. Choose the answer that is the best way to write the underlined section. If the passage is correctly punctuated, mark the oval beside *No mistake*.

(1) Do you want to plan a healthful lunch menu together? asked Mrs. McMann. (2) "We could prepare it together."

(3) "Could we have carrots" asked Kim. (4) "We should make a big salad!" exclaimed Tom. "I love salad. (5) What should we put in it"

(6) "Carrots," said Rabe "are good when they are grated."

(7) "so are radishes," said Betsy.

1. ◉ Add quotation marks around direct quote.
   ○ Add comma before *asked*.
   ○ Capitalize *asked*.
   ○ No mistake

2. ○ Remove quotation mark after *together*.
   ○ Place comma at end of quote.
   ○ Begin a new paragraph.
   ◉ No mistake

3. ○ Place comma after *Kim*.
   ◉ Place question mark at end of quote.
   ○ Place period at end of quote.
   ○ No mistake

4. ○ Capitalize *exclaimed*.
   ○ Place comma after *Tom*.
   ◉ Begin a new paragraph.
   ○ No mistake

5. ◉ Place question mark after direct quote.
   ○ Place period after direct quote.
   ○ Add quotation marks before *What*.
   ○ No mistake

6. ◉ Place comma after *Rabe*.
   ○ Place exclamation point after *carrots*.
   ○ Capitalize *are*.
   ○ No mistake

7. ○ Remove quotation marks after *radishes*.
   ○ Replace comma with period.
   ◉ Capitalize *so*.
   ○ No mistake

Practice • More About Quotation Marks

Name _____

Easily Confused Words: Homophones

A. Write each underlined homophone correctly.

1. <u>Your</u> sure to stay healthy if you eat well
   and exercise every day, <u>two</u>. _____You're; too_____

2. <u>Its</u> important to have certain vitamins. _____It's_____

3. <u>Their</u> is vitamin C in a baked potato. _____There_____

4. My cousins should change <u>they're</u> eating habits. _____their_____

5. <u>Too</u> servings of fruit a day is not quite enough. _____Two_____

B. Write each sentence below. Choose the correct word in parentheses to complete each sentence.

6. I have **(heard, herd)** sailors had to eat sprouts and drink citrus juice.
   I have heard sailors had to eat sprouts and drink citrus juice.

7. They did not have any fresh fruit or vegetables **(four, for)** months.
   They did not have any fresh fruit or vegetables for months.

8. Many diseases can be prevented with the **(write, right)** vitamins.
   Many diseases can be prevented with the right vitamins.

9. **(One, Won)** piece of fruit a day would have prevented their illness.
   One piece of fruit a day would have prevented their illness.

10. Now we **(no, know)** they were lacking vitamins in their diets.
    Now we know they were lacking vitamins in their diets.

TRY THIS! Write four sentences about the food you like. Use four of the following words in your sentences: *for, four, won, one, right, write, knew,* and *new.*

Name _____

Negatives

A. Write the negative in each sentence.

1. Uncle Alex never skips his oatmeal in the morning. _____never_____

2. He doesn't like to eat before he jogs. _____doesn't_____

3. Nobody in the family can run as he does. _____Nobody_____

4. Sammy won't eat butter on his toast. _____won't_____

5. Neither will I. _____Neither_____

B. Use one word from the box to complete each sentence and make it negative. You may use a word more than once.

| no | none | nobody | never | not | nothing |

6. Most candy does __not__ have minerals, either.

7. Our teacher told us that plain sugar has __none__.

8. I __never__ eat sugar without brushing my teeth afterward.

9. My family does __not__ have dessert every night.

10. Sometimes we have oranges, and sometimes we have __nothing__ at all.

11. __Nobody__ needs to eat candy every day.

12. My father has __no__ sugar in his tea.

TRY THIS! Write a few sentences about some fruits or parts of fruits you don't eat. Use negatives from the box on this page.

Practice • Negatives and Easily Confused Words   Unit 6 • Chapter 35   117

Name _____

Avoiding Double Negatives

A. Each sentence contains a double negative. Write each negative sentence correctly.

1. There aren't no apples left.

   There aren't any apples left. OR There are no apples left.

2. I didn't take no vitamins yesterday.

   I didn't take any vitamins yesterday. OR I took no vitamins yesterday.

3. Your body doesn't need no sweets.

   Your body doesn't need any sweets. OR Your body needs no sweets.

4. I never knew nobody who hated raisins.

   I never knew anybody (OR I knew nobody) who hated raisins.

5. Won't you never stop eating potato chips?

   Will you never stop (OR Won't you ever stop) eating potato chips?

B. Circle the word or words that best complete each negative sentence.

6. Molly never eats (no, **any**) bread.

7. She (**does not**, does not never) forget to study health guides.

8. There is (**never anything**, almost never nothing) wrong with her health.

9. (Not nobody, **Nobody**) else in the family is a vegetarian.

10. They (**would never**, wouldn't never) give up their hamburgers!

TRY THIS! Write three reasons why you would or would not be a vegetarian. Use negatives in each of your sentences. Make sure you do not use double negatives.

118 Unit 6 • Chapter 35   Practice • Negatives and Easily Confused Words

Name _____

Extra Practice

A. Each sentence contains a homophone error. Write each sentence correctly.

1. Its a good idea to eat a healthful breakfast every day.
   It's a good idea to eat a healthful breakfast every day.

2. My mother was write about the grapefruit.
   My mother was right about the grapefruit.

3. She new it would taste sweet enough without sugar.
   She knew it would taste sweet enough without sugar.

4. They're was an extra half of a grapefruit on the table.
   There was an extra half of a grapefruit on the table.

5. I ate it and drank orange juice, two.
   I ate it and drank orange juice, too.

B. If a sentence contains a double negative, draw an X on the extra negative word. If the sentence is correct, write *Correct*.

6. Cereals contain fiber and vitamins. — *Correct*

7. Frank doesn't ~~never~~ get any exercise. — ___

8. Your heart will not be ~~no~~ good without exercise. — ___

9. Nobody can have ~~no~~ strong muscles without exercise. — ___

10. Muscles will not grow without good nutrition. — *Correct*

TRY THIS! Plan a healthful breakfast. Write what you will eat and what you will not eat and why. Use at least three negatives and three homophones in your writing.

Practice • Negatives and Easily Confused Words   Unit 6 • Chapter 35   119

Name _____

Chapter Review

Read the passage. Choose the correct word for each numbered space. Fill in the oval next to your choice.

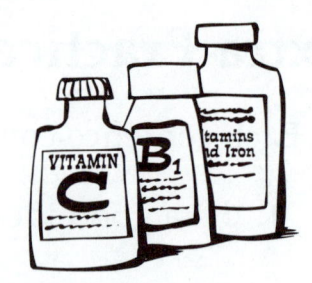

In 1912, __(1)__ was a scientist who wrote about "vitamines." He said that some vitamins dissolve in water and others dissolve in fat. Other scientists agreed he was __(2)__. Soon people began to understand that vitamins could prevent disease. Today, most people understand that vitamins are __(3)__ necessary for your health. It's not __(4)__ problem to find vitamins. We can go __(5)__ a market and buy fresh vegetables, grains, and fruits all year round. Doctors do not __(6)__ have to __(7)__ a prescription __(8)__ most kinds of vitamins.

1. ○ there
   ○ they're
   ○ their
   ○ the

2. ○ right
   ○ write
   ○ rite
   ○ Wright

3. ○ not
   ○ never
   ○ truly
   ○ nothing

4. ○ no
   ○ never
   ○ a
   ○ neither

5. ○ two
   ○ to
   ○ too
   ○ toe

6. ○ ever
   ○ never
   ○ neither
   ○ no

7. ○ right
   ○ Wright
   ○ rite
   ○ write

8. ○ four
   ○ for
   ○ fore
   ○ neither

120 Unit 6 • Chapter 35   Practice • Negatives and Easily Confused Words

UNIT 1

Grammar • Sentences
Writing • Expressive Writing

Name _____

My Trip to the Big City
by Roy Hauser

I was born and raised in a very small town. Everyone here knows each other. It is hard not to, since the entire population is only 87 people. That is just 17 families. Not much ever happens in this town. It is as quiet as a whisper all year round. You can imagine how excited my friends were to hear that my family was going to visit the big city for the holidays.

1

Imagery

Think about an enjoyable place that you visited. It might be in your community or elsewhere. Make notes on the things that you remember most. Use vivid words that will form pictures in your reader's mind.

Notes

_____
_____
_____

Remember that imagery makes writing more descriptive and interesting. Using your notes, write sentences that tell about the place that you remember so well. Use vivid language to describe how things looked and how they made you feel.

_____
_____
_____
_____

Family Note: After your child reads the personal narrative, talk about a place you have visited together. Discuss your most vivid memories of the place.

8

Practice • Take-Home Book 1

Unit 1   121

Before we left, it seemed as though everyone in town had some kind of advice for me. Don't talk to strangers in the big city. Don't stare up at tall buildings. Don't walk alone. With all those "don'ts," I began to wonder what I should *do* when I reached the city.

2

With Dad's permission, I proudly took the woman's arm and helped her across the street. When we reached the other side, she squeezed my hand and smiled. "Thank you so much, sonny," she said. "You know, people appreciate small kindnesses."

Later, I shared many memories with my friends and neighbors. However, the memory of that woman's words will stick with me most of all.

7

We arrived by bus early in the afternoon. Wow! What sights I saw! The city was like a giant machine with all its parts moving loudly at once. On the sidewalks, crowds of people snaked from corner to corner. In the street, a stream of cars, buses, and cabs paraded along. Their horns were a symphony of beeps, honks, and toots. I had never heard anything like it in my life.

Armies of busy people marched past the woman. No one seemed to notice her, as though she were invisible. When the woman looked up, her sad eyes met mine. I tugged on my father's sleeve and said, "That woman needs help, Dad."

We walked to the corner, and I smiled at the woman. "Do you need help?" I asked.

"Oh, thank you, sonny," the woman sighed. "If you could just escort me across the street."

I held my father's hand tightly as we squeezed through the crowds. My mother stopped us along the way to look at the store windows. They were beautiful, giant picture postcards. One window had large plastic figures that looked just like real people. They were dressed in bright red coats and gold scarves. Another window had large toy animals on display. It was like a colorful zoo that had come to life!

As I stared at one large window, I saw something from the corner of my eye. It was not anything in the store display, however. It was someone on the street. I turned around and there she was. Standing at the corner was an elderly woman. She was bundled in a heavy coat. She leaned on a small shopping cart that was full of groceries. She stared sadly ahead as cars and trucks whipped by in the street.

UNIT 2

Grammar • More About Nouns and Verbs
Writing • Informative Writing

Name _____

Watch Them Grow
by LaToya Richards

(mold — lemon)

Not all plants are green and leafy. Molds belong to a group of plants called fungi. They have no seeds, no leaves, and no substances that make them green. Molds do grow, however, and it can be both fun and interesting to watch them grow. You can do your own experiment to see where and how molds grow.

1

Ordering Ideas

Plan a how-to paragraph about making a salad. Use the pictures here to help you, or think of your own ingredients. List the steps in time order.

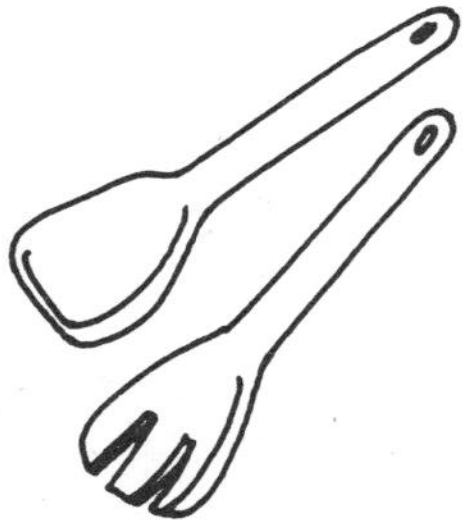

carrots
celery
lettuce
peppers
salad servers
salad dressing
salad bowl

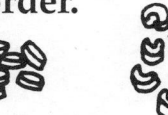

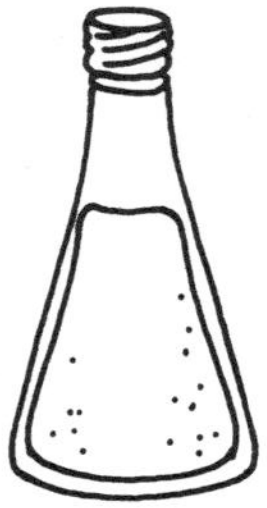

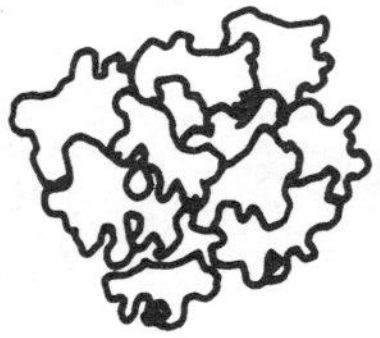

_____
_____
_____
_____
_____

Family Note: Have your child read the how-to essay about growing molds. Help your child recall other scientific experiments he or she might have performed or seen.

8

Practice • Take-Home Book 2

Unit 2   125

You will need only a few basic materials for this experiment. Get a large, clean jar with a screw-on lid. The jar can be glass or plastic. It should be clear so that you can see into it. Be sure you have permission to use the jar. After you complete the experiment, you will have to throw it away. You will also need some adhesive tape and about one cup of water in a paper cup. In addition, you should have paper and a pencil for taking notes about your observations.

2

Keep watching the changes in your molds. Write notes about the changes you see. After about two weeks, it's time to end your experiment. Throw the jar away without opening it. Keep your notes and drawings or photographs, though. They are a good reminder of your experiment with growing molds.

7

126 Unit 2

Practice • Take-Home Book 2

The most important materials for this experiment are several pieces of leftover food. Get permission to use these foods, too. They will have to be thrown away at the end of the experiment. Choose different kinds of foods. For example, you might choose an orange segment, part of a carrot, a small piece of bread, a bit of cheese, and part of a cookie. Do not use leftovers that include meat or fish.

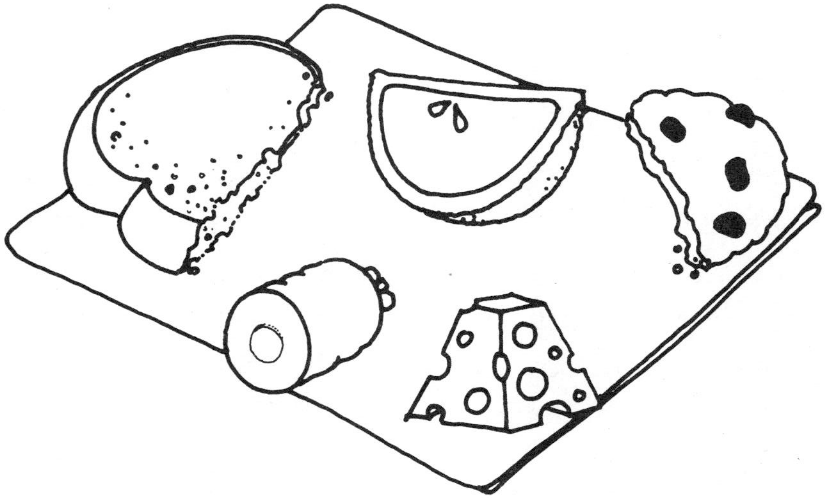

3

Be patient. For two or three days, you may not see any changes. The first signs of molds growing might look like dust. As the days pass, however, you will probably notice several different kinds of molds. Some may look blue, others green, and still others white. Look for differences in texture, too.

Watch to see where molds grow first. Notice how quickly different molds grow and whether some molds spread from one food to another.

6

Practice • Take-Home Book 2

Unit 2   127

After you have gathered all the materials, you can begin the experiment. First, lay the jar on its side. Then quickly dip each piece of food into the water in the paper cup. Place the food inside the jar. Spread the pieces of food out. The pieces can touch, but do not crowd them together in one part of the jar.

Screw the lid tightly onto the jar. Then wrap a piece of tape around the edge of the lid to seal it.

Keep your sealed jar on its side. Make sure that no one can accidentally knock your jar over or throw it away. Place it in an out-of-the-way spot. Put a sign in front of the jar.

DO NOT DISTURB!
MOLDS ARE GROWING HERE.

Every day, look at the food in your jar. Make notes about what you see. Draw pictures showing what you see. You might even take photographs or use colored pencils to make detailed drawings.

UNIT 3

Grammar • **More About Verbs**
Writing • **Persuasive Writing**

Name _____

Learn to Cartoon
by Susan Kinney

Draw an oval. Then draw three small circles, some curved lines, and a few squiggles. You've done it! You have created a funny cartoon face. With practice, anyone can learn to draw cartoons. Cartooning might seem easy, but that does not mean it is not important. Cartooning has so many advantages that everyone should learn to cartoon.

1

Capturing a Reader's Interest

Think of sentences that will grab and hold a reader's interest in each of these cartoons. Write a sentence about each.

_____

_____

_____

_____

_____

_____

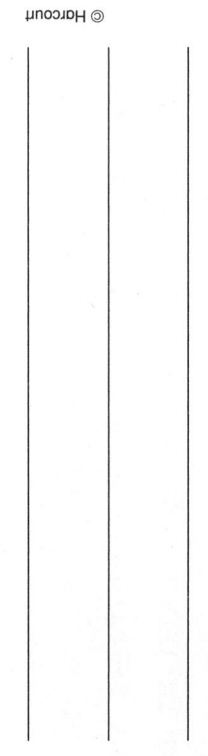

Family Note: Have your child read the persuasive essay. Together, discuss cartoons your child might enjoy drawing. Also discuss any cartoon strips or editorial cartoons your child might have seen in newspapers or magazines.

8

Practice • Take-Home Book 3

Unit 3   129

Cartooning can help you express yourself. Your cartoons show your own ideas and feelings. Are you impressed by a dog's long tail? Then you can make that dog's tail the most important part of your cartoon. Others might make the dog's ears or eyes the most important part. In your cartoons, though, *you* make your own decisions. You also get to use your imagination. How do you think the dog might look riding a bike? You can show that in a cartoon, too.

2

As you can see, cartooning really is an important skill. It can help you express yourself, organize your ideas, and learn about art materials while you have a good time. So hurry to your library, find a few good books on drawing cartoons, grab a pencil, and get started. Then have fun cartooning!

7

130 Unit 3

Practice • Take-Home Book 3

Cartooning also helps you organize your ideas. As you plan and draw a cartoon, you should ask yourself questions like these: *What is most important here? Which details are worth including? Which details will not help me create the simple, funny picture I want to draw?* Sorting your ideas in this way is an important skill. You use it when you make plans, when you study, and even when you write stories and essays.

3

Cartooning is quick and fun. You don't need to be a talented artist to draw good cartoons. You don't need fancy art materials, either. Some of the best cartoons are drawn with pencil on scraps of paper. With a few fast lines, you can express your ideas and make your friends laugh.

6

Practice • Take-Home Book 3

Unit 3   131

When you draw cartoons, you have a chance to learn more about art materials. Of course, you will probably use pencils to draw your first cartoons. Then you can experiment with pens, crayons, and markers for color. Later, you might try paints, charcoal, pastels, and calligraphy pens. You might try different kinds of paper, too. You will find that different art materials give your cartoons different looks.

4

© Harcourt

After some practice, you can use your cartooning skills in many ways. You can draw cartoon notes for your friends and make greeting cards with your own cartoon characters. You can also draw cartoon strips to tell stories.

You might make cartooning your career. Some cartoonists draw comic strips. Others draw political cartoons for the editorial section of a newspaper. Still others work in teams making animated movies.

5

132 Unit 3

Practice • Take-Home Book 3

UNIT 4

- **Grammar**: Pronouns, Adjectives, and Adverbs
- **Writing**: Informative Writing (Classification)

Name _____

My Life as a Dinosaur Expert
by Kyle Ortiz

It started slowly. In first grade, I was just like the other students. We could all identify pictures of a T-Rex, an apatosaurus, and a stegosaurus. We all knew that a triceratops had three horns. By second grade, most of my friends had forgotten all about dinosaurs, but I was still fascinated by them. I went on learning about dinosaurs, thinking about them, and talking about them. Now I am known as an expert. There are some terrific advantages to being a dinosaur expert, but there are a few disadvantages, too.

1

Powerful Words

Think of some powerful words you could use to describe each of these animals. Write your powerful words in the boxes.

Family Note: Ask your child to read the essay. Does your child think of himself or herself as an expert on a certain topic? Discuss the special interests your child has.

8

Practice • Take-Home Book 4

Unit 4 133

One of the best parts of being a dinosaur expert is answering questions and helping other people learn about my favorite subject. Of course, the first graders like to ask me questions. I enjoy talking with them and showing them interesting pictures in one of my books. Classmates sometimes ask me about dinosaurs. Every now and then, my teacher has a question, too. I feel happy to be the person with the answers!

2

I have been a dinosaur expert for several years. I hope to be one for a long, long time. In spite of a few disadvantages, I enjoy the advantages that come with being an expert.

7

134 Unit 4

Practice • Take-Home Book 4

Because I am a dinosaur expert, I always get presents I like. No one ever has to ask what I want for my birthday or other special occasions. The answer is always dinosaur books, dinosaur posters, dinosaur models, anything to do with dinosaurs! For me, this is a terrific advantage. I am always happy to get something new about dinosaurs.

3

Another disadvantage to being a dinosaur expert comes after I fall asleep. I like daydreaming about dinosaurs when I am awake. However, I would rather dream about something small, quiet, and peaceful at night. Too often, the biggest, fiercest dinosaurs show up in my dreams. I wish they would stay inside those books I enjoy so much!

6

Practice • Take-Home Book 4

Unit 4 135

Another advantage of being a dinosaur expert is that I am never bored. When I have to wait in a doctor's office, I am happy just to daydream. I review the names of dinosaurs and recall the differences between a diplodocus and a barosaurus. In my mind, I see a lesothosaurus running across the plains. I picture an Edmontosaurus herd grazing. Dinosaurs are always interesting companions for me.

Of course, being a dinosaur expert has its drawbacks. One problem is that my half of the bedroom is very crowded. Dinosaur posters cover my walls, and dinosaur books and models fill my bookcase. Part of the floor is covered with large dinosaur models, too. My older brother, a sports-car expert, sometimes groans that my dinosaurs are taking over.

UNIT 5

Grammar • **Phrases and Clauses**
Writing • **Research Report**

Name _____

The White House
by Anna Clemens

Tourists from around the world enjoy visiting Washington, D.C., our nation's capital. They want to see many different buildings, monuments, and statues. Most Washington tourists are especially interested in seeing the White House, the office and home of the American President.

1

Topic Sentence and Details

Plan an informative paragraph about an interesting building. It might be a building you have visited, one you have seen on TV or one you have read about. Use this web to show your ideas for the paragraph. In the middle of the web, write a topic sentence that tells your main idea. In the other spaces, write details about the main idea.

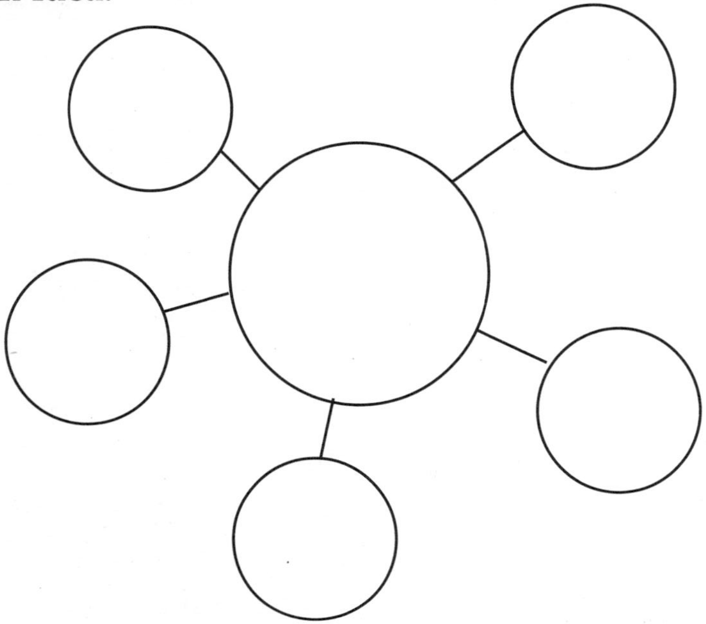

Family Note: Have your child read the research report about the White House. Together, discuss historic sites that members of your family have visited or would like to visit.

8

Practice • Take-Home Book 5

Unit 5   137

History of the White House

The White House was designed by James Hoban. Workers began building the house in 1792, while George Washington was President. It was not ready until 1800, when John Adams was President. Adams and his family moved into the White House, even though only six rooms of the building were finished.

In 1814, British soldiers set fire to the White House. When the fire was put out, only the outside walls were left. It took three years to rebuild the White House.

As both the office and the home of our President, the White House is one of the most important buildings in the country. It is also a beautiful building, filled with reminders about the history of the United States. A tour of the White House can be the highlight of any visit to Washington, D.C.

At first, the official name of the building was "the President's House." Later the official name was changed to the "Executive Mansion." However, many people simply referred to it as the White House. In 1901 President Theodore Roosevelt made the "White House" the official name of the building.

Rooms of the White House

The White House is a large, impressive building. It has six floors, including two basements. There are 132 rooms, three elevators, and seven staircases.

White House Tours

Visitors can tour the public rooms of the White House on Tuesday through Saturday between 10 in the morning and noon. Their first stop is usually the nearby White House Visitor Center, where they can watch a short movie about the White House and look at exhibits. Once in the White House, visitors usually move on their own through the five public rooms. Secret Service Tour Officers are available to answer questions.

The ground floor of the White House includes several rooms that are open to tourists on a regular schedule. These rooms are also used by the President and the First Lady for official functions. The largest is the East Room, which has been used for dances, receptions, and concerts. The State Dining Room is large enough for dinner parties with 140 guests. Green silk covers the walls of the Green Room, and the walls of the Red Room are covered in red satin. Receptions are often held in the Blue Room, which has an oval shape.

Other rooms on the ground floor and upper floors of the White House are used by the President, the Presidential staff, and family members. Like the Blue Room, the office where the President works has an oval shape. It is called the Oval Office. The ground floor also includes the kitchen, a library, and several other offices. Upstairs are living rooms and bedrooms for the President and his family, as well as for guests and for staff members.

UNIT 6

- **Grammar**
- **Usage and Mechanics**
- **Writing**
- **Expressive Writing: Folktale**

Name _____

Bear's Special Gift
by Joseph Chang

In a tall forest far away lived a friendly and adorable Bear. Every morning he came out of his cozy, warm cave and sniffed the crisp, cool mountain air. Then he greeted all his forest neighbors.

"Good morning, my good friends," Bear growled in his sweetest voice.

"Good morning, Bear," everyone replied.

1

Using Sensory Details

Think about something that you like to do, such as play basketball, sing, or paint. Make notes on what happens when you do the activity. Use sensory details—words that appeal to the sense of sight, hearing, touch, smell, or taste.

Notes

_____
_____
_____
_____

Sensory details make writing more interesting. Using your notes, write sentences about the thing you like to do. Use sensory details.

_____
_____
_____
_____

Family Note: After your child reads the folktale, talk about special talents that you and other family members have. Discuss ways in which you put your talents to use.

8

Practice • Take-Home Book 6

Unit 6 141

One morning Bear watched Woodpecker as she pecked holes in a tree. Rat-a-tat-tat! Rat-a-tat-tat! "That looks like great fun," Bear said thoughtfully. "I would like to peck holes, too." Bear stood in front of the tall, thick tree and began to push his nose at the bark.

"Ouch!" Bear cried. "Pecking at a tree is not at all fun for me. My nose is simply too stubby and too tender."

Now Bear felt deeply sad. "Each of my friends can do something special," he moaned. "But I have no such gift. I'm just a plain, ordinary, average bear."

Bear sat, quietly thinking. Suddenly he came alive.

"I know what I can do!" Bear shouted. "I know my gift! I can give each of my forest friends a big, friendly bear hug!"

That is just what he did, every morning and every night.

Later, as Bear walked through the forest, he stopped to watch Snake exercise. Snake coiled his body and stretched until his head actually touched the tip of his tail.

"I'll bet I can do that!" Bear said cheerfully. Bear looked to the left and stretched his thick, furry neck as far as it would go. Sadly, that wasn't very far.

"Oh, dear," Bear sighed heavily. "I guess I can't coil and stretch like Snake after all."

3

Soon, Elephant came out to exercise. He lifted a huge, heavy tree log with his curled-up trunk. "Move over, Elephant!" Bear said firmly. "I can lift just as well as you!"

Bear found a huge log and tried to balance it on his head. The log crashed to the forest floor.

"Well, it *looked* easy," Bear said with disappointment.

6

Practice • Take-Home Book 6

Unit 6 143

Just then, Bear saw Kangaroo hop high over an old tree stump.

"Now, I'm *sure* I can do that," Bear said confidently. He stood before the stump and tried to spring over it. To his great surprise, he landed flat on top of the stump instead.

"I guess I can't leap as high as Kangaroo," Bear grumbled.

Next, Peacock strutted by and fanned out his long, blue-green feathers. What a beautiful spread of colors appeared!

"What a magnificent display!" Bear gasped. "I must do that, too. I must fan out my feathers right away!"

How disappointed Bear was to discover that he had no feathers to fan.

"I'm all fur," he sighed heavily. "No feathers, no fan, no fun."

Skills Index

GRAMMAR

Adjectives, 71–80
Adverbs, 71–80
Nouns, 6–10, 21–30
    more about nouns, 21–25
    possessive nouns, 26–30
    subjects, 6–10
Prepositions, 81–85
Pronouns, 61–70
Sentences, 1–5, 16–20, 86–100
    complex sentences, 91–95
    phrases and clauses, 86–90
    sentence fragments and run-on sentences, 96–100
    sentences, 1–5
    simple and compound sentences, 16–20
Verbs, 11–15, 31–60
    action verbs and linking verbs, 31–35
    future-tense verbs, 51–55
    irregular verbs, 56–60
    main verbs and helping verbs, 36–40
    past-tense verbs, 46–50
    predicates, 11–15
    present-tense verbs, 41–45

Skills Index

USAGE AND MECHANICS

Abbreviations, 23
Apostrophes, 38, 39
Be, 32–35
Combining Sentence Parts, 8, 13, 18
Colons, 102–105
Commas, 93, 101–105
Contractions, 38
Easily Confused Words, 116–120
Exclamation Point, 2, 3
Hyphens, 108
Negatives, 117–120
Periods, 1–5
Pronoun-Antecedent Agreement, 61
Question Marks, 3
Quotation Marks, 106–115
Subject-Verb Agreement, 43, 48
Titles, 106–107, 109–110

ASSESSMENT

Test Preparation, 5, 10, 15, 20, 25, 30, 35, 40, 45, 50, 55, 60, 65, 70, 75, 80, 85, 90, 95, 100, 105, 110, 115, 120